RHS

PLANTS
from
PIPS

RHS Plants from Pips

Author: Holly Farrell

First published in Great Britain in 2015 by Mitchell Beazley, an imprint of

Octopus Publishing Group Ltd, Endeavour House, 189 Shaftesbury Avenue, London WC2H 8JY

www.octopusbooks.co.uk

A Hachette UK Company

www.hachette.co.uk

Published in association with the Royal Horticultural Society

ISBN: 978 1 78472 044 5

A CIP record of this book is available from the British Library

Set in Gill Sans and Madurai Slab

Printed and bound in China

Mitchell Beazley Publisher: Alison Starling

RHS Publisher: Rae Spencer Jones

Conceived, designed and produced by

Quid Publishing

Level 4 Sheridan House

Hove BN3 1DD

England

Cover design: Clare Barber

Designer: Clare Barber

Illustrations: Melvyn Evans

RHS consultant editor: Simon Maughan

The Royal Horticultural Society is the UK's leading gardening charity dedicated to advancing
horticulture and promoting good gardening. Its charitable work includes providing expert advice
and information, training the next generation of gardeners, creating hands-on opportunities for
children to grow plants and conducting research into plants, pests and environmental issues
affecting gardeners.

For more information visit www.rhs.org.uk or call 0845 130 4646.

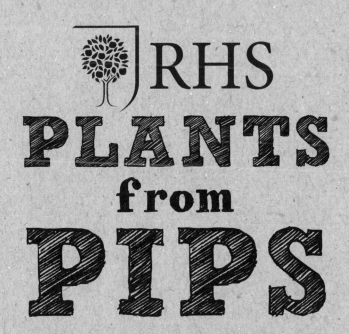

RHS PLANTS from PIPS

Pots of Plants for the Whole Family to Enjoy

Holly Farrell

MITCHELL
BEAZLEY

CONTENTS

CHAPTER 4:
LOOKING AFTER PLANTS AS THEY GROW...114

INTRODUCTION

How often have you looked at a pile of fruit pips and thought 'I wonder if they would grow?', before consigning them to the dustbin? The truth is, they probably would grow – and more easily than you think.

Growing plants from pips is fun, requires very little equipment or outlay – most of what is needed can be found in the kitchen – and can be done indoors, all year round. Growing a pip is a great project for anyone interested in starting gardening in a small way, even without a garden. It is also a brilliant means of introducing children to the outdoors and the science of plants.

No previous gardening experience is necessary, only enthusiasm and a little patience. How to grow each pip is described in foolproof detail, backed up with general advice on the basics of looking after plants.

A pip could produce an unusual houseplant like the date palm, or it could create a new variety of apple or raspberry (why not give it a name yourself?). Whichever pips you choose to grow, the excitement of seeing the first shoots appear, and the satisfaction of raising a plant from a pip, are hard to beat.

So before you throw away those pips, remember, all you need is a pot and a windowsill, and you could do something interesting with them instead.

HOW TO USE THIS BOOK

This book includes everything you need to know about pips and how to grow them – from the anatomy of a single pip, to how to grow specific fruits. It's not necessary to read it from cover to cover: perhaps start with growing a single type of pip, then return to find out more information about the science of pips at a later date and try something more adventurous.

Chapter 1 explains what pips are and how they grow, and what to expect when growing pips at home.

Chapter 2 gives general information on how to start off growing pips and the basic equipment that is needed. Use this chapter in conjunction with the specific information for each pip in Chapter 3.

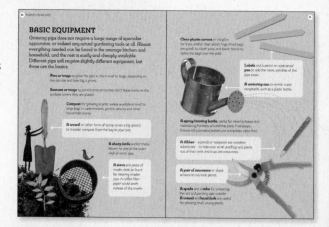

Chapter 3 is about each pip in detail. It includes pips from exotic fruit that will grow into interesting houseplants, pips from vegetables that could be grown inside or out, and pips from fruit that will happily grow outdoors.

KEY TO GROWING PIPS

EASINESS: 🌢 very easy 🌢🌢 moderate 🌢🌢🌢 some skill required

PATIENCE: 🌢 fast growing 🌢🌢 needs more time 🌢🌢🌢 grows into a tree.

Chapter 4 contains information on looking after the pips as they grow, and what to do if anything goes wrong. As with Chapter 2, use this as a general guide but also refer to the specifics for each pip in Chapter 3.

Finally, the Glossary explains technical terms, and the Further Resources section gives some sources of more information.

CHAPTER 1
HOW PLANTS GROW

Growing plants from pips is a fun and easy way to start gardening, with results that are much more interesting than the average houseplant. Gardening is not really as difficult or complicated as you might think: plants want to grow and prosper, and all the gardener needs to do is to provide them with a suitable situation in which to do so.

This chapter will help you get started by explaining the inner workings of a pip and what happens to it once it is in that pot on the windowsill. You'll find out how plants spread their pips in the wild and what to expect from the pips as they grow. You're going to need a little patience, but the results will make it all worthwhile!

WHAT ARE PIPS?

A pip is a seed contained within a fruit or vegetable. Larger pips are sometimes called stones. Botanically, a fruit is the ovary of the plant, containing the seed(s), but is generally defined as the whole structure, including any edible flesh around the seeds. Many items commonly called vegetables, such as tomatoes, are therefore technically fruits.

PLANT REPRODUCTION

A plant has two main means of reproducing itself in order to perpetuate its species. It can clone itself (vegetative reproduction) or produce seeds (sexual reproduction).

There are many types of vegetative reproduction, and one such example is layering, when a plant's branch or stem makes roots where it bends to touch the ground, and ultimately grows away into a separate plant that would survive if the original plant died. Some plants can grow into new plants if a piece of their root is severed and left in the ground. Gardeners exploit the means by which plants can reproduce themselves to create new plants, for example by cuttings, where new plants can be grown from a piece of severed root or stem.

Vegetative reproduction, however, is not always useful to the gardener, and many plants that do this aggressively are classed as weeds, for example bindweed and Japanese knotweed.

Seeds are embryonic plants, made when a flower is pollinated. Female flowers possess an ovary containing eggs. When pollen from a male flower lands in the centre of the female flower – brought by insects, animals, the wind or water – it stimulates the growth of pollen tubes down into the ovary, which develops into a seed or cluster of seeds.

Producing seeds uses a lot of the plant's energy, but it means that a plant species is able to spread further afield. Since the offspring are not exact clones of their parents, it allows for the evolution of new characteristics that may help the species to survive. Plants often flower when under heavy stress, such as drought, in order to make seeds that will go on to survive even if the original plant dies.

WHAT'S INSIDE A PIP?

A pip contains within it everything the plant will need to start growing a tiny root, a shoot bearing the first leaf/leaves and a store of energy to push the root and shoot out of the casing and into the world.

ANATOMY OF A SEED

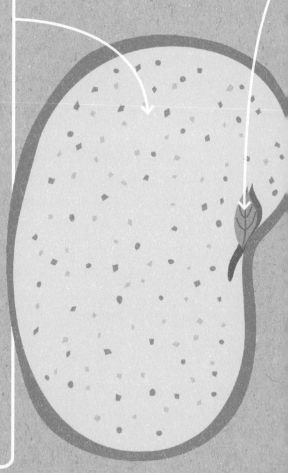

Cotyledons. The cotyledons are stores of food and nutrients that the developing embryo uses up during germination. The energy is mostly in the form of carbohydrates (starch), but also sometimes fats/oils (such as in nuts and sunflowers, for example). As the seedling uses the energy in the cotyledons to grow, they shrink and die off.

Sometimes known as the 'seed leaves', these are normally the first pair of leaves that plants will put above the soil surface after germination. Botanists classify plants by how many seed leaves they have: one seed leaf (monocotyledenous) is characteristic of, for example, grasses; most flowering plants have two seed leaves (dicotyledenous). Most of the pips are dicotyledenous, but some, such as the date palm, are monocotyledenous.

Embryo. The new plant in miniature, it consists of a tiny root (radicle) and shoot (plumule), connected by a structure called the hypocotyl. The plumule consists of a short section of stem and the first proper, or 'true', leaves.

Seed coat. This is the skin of the seed, containing and protecting the embryo and energy stores. The thickness varies widely between species; how thick the seed coat is will determine how easily it absorbs water to trigger germination. It sometimes also contains chemicals to inhibit germination until specific environmental conditions are met. Generally, the colour is a shade of brown, to camouflage the seed against the soil and protect it from being eaten.

SEEDS WITH AN ENDOSPERM

Endosperm. Some plants have an additional store of energy to use during germination called the endosperm. This varies in size between different species: for some plants the cotyledons are the primary store and the endosperm is tiny, for others the endosperm is the main source of energy.

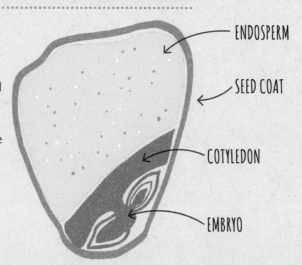

ENDOSPERM

SEED COAT

COTYLEDON

EMBRYO

HOW PLANTS SPREAD THEIR PIPS

The next step for the plant is to spread its seeds far and wide, hopefully to a piece of ground suitable for growth and where the new seedlings will not be in competition with the original plant. Different plants have evolved different mechanisms for dispersing their seeds.

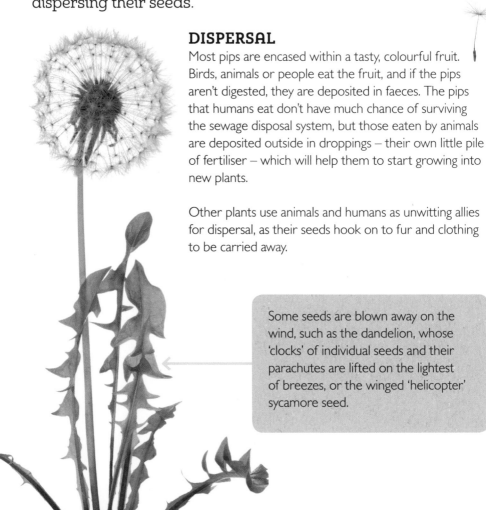

DISPERSAL

Most pips are encased within a tasty, colourful fruit. Birds, animals or people eat the fruit, and if the pips aren't digested, they are deposited in faeces. The pips that humans eat don't have much chance of surviving the sewage disposal system, but those eaten by animals are deposited outside in droppings – their own little pile of fertiliser – which will help them to start growing into new plants.

Other plants use animals and humans as unwitting allies for dispersal, as their seeds hook on to fur and clothing to be carried away.

Some seeds are blown away on the wind, such as the dandelion, whose 'clocks' of individual seeds and their parachutes are lifted on the lightest of breezes, or the winged 'helicopter' sycamore seed.

A few plants (e.g. gorse) literally explode their seeds out into the world from a pod that bursts open when the seeds are ready.

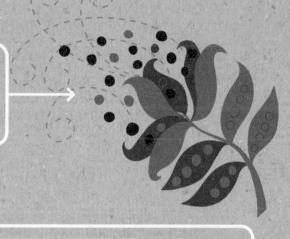

Water can sometimes carry seeds, such as the coconut, many hundreds of miles before they are washed on to shore and germinate.

DORMANCY

The seed must then wait for the optimum conditions to germinate. Before they are taken away from the plant, the seeds ripen, losing 85–90 per cent of their moisture content as they dry. Once dry/ripe they will remain dormant until the conditions are just right for them to germinate.

Again, the mechanisms for maintaining the seed in a dormant state vary from species to species, with most employing at least one method and some a combination of different methods to ensure the seed will only start to grow once it has the best chance of survival.

The types of dormancy affecting the pips, and the means of breaking them, are detailed on pages 42–43.

DO NOT DISTURB

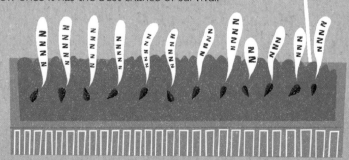

HOW PIPS GROW

Germination can be a mysterious and frustrating process for the gardener. Having buried the pip in the soil, there is no way to know if anything is happening until that first miraculous shoot or root appears out of the pot.

Provided the pip is viable (that is, it contains everything it needs to grow and is not too old), its dormancy has been broken, and that it is in adequately aerated and moist soil in the correct temperature range, the next thing that happens is that the pip begins to take in water.

Tiny holes in the seed coat allow water to penetrate and the pip begins to swell, breaking open the seed coat to allow more water to be absorbed. Oxygen from air pockets in the soil can also now be taken into the seed, where it is used in chemical reactions to break down the stored energy sources of starch and fats into sugars.

The embryo uses these sugars as energy to make new cells, lengthening the radicle and pushing it out into the soil. It anchors the seed in the soil, and soon branches out to spread in different directions in search of water and nutrients to absorb.

It is only once the stem and leaves emerge into the light that the plant is able to stop relying on the energy stored in the seed and start manufacturing its own food. Under the soil the stem and leaves are white, but once they emerge and unfold they quickly turn green. Chemical reactions, under the genetic direction of each cell nucleus, are occurring to make chlorophyll, which allows the plant to begin the process of photosynthesis (see pages 26–27).

The embryonic shoot is also developing, pushing up through the soil towards the light. The stem is hooked, and the bend of the hook emerges first, straightening once it has broken the surface to pull the leaves up through the soil and into the light.

GROWING FROM PIPS

Growing pips is a fun and interesting project, but it is important to know what to expect. Potential pip-growers should not be dissuaded: follow the instructions and have a little patience and the pips will grow into amazing plants.

WHAT TO EXPECT

Many of the tropical fruits grown from pips indoors are unlikely to bear fruit in cooler climates (although it is not impossible), but will nonetheless make great houseplants.

Outside, fruit on the trees grown from pips will not necessarily be the same variety as the fruit that it came from. For example, a pip from a Braeburn apple will grow an apple tree that has characteristics of Braeburns, but also of the other varieties by which the original tree was pollinated. The same is true of vegetables, although because the variety range tends to be smaller, the differences from the original vegetable will be less pronounced.

Tree fruit will also take some time to grow – it may be years before they bear fruit.

CHAPTER 2

HOW TO GROW PLANTS SUCCESSFULLY

This chapter covers everything you need to know about how to start growing plants from pips and gives solid advice on how to be a successful gardener. The best foundation for growing plants well is a basic understanding of their biology and an appreciation of the conditions they will prefer given where they grow in the wild. Green fingers are not necessary; just simple equipment, much of which can be kitchen implements or recycled food packaging.

The science behind plant growth and its relevance to the gardener is explained here. Then the whole process is covered – gathering the pips, what to grow them in, where and how to plant them, then how to care for them as they begin to grow.

GATHERING THE PIPS

The beauty of growing from pips is that the fruit and vegetables they come from are widely available to buy from supermarkets, greengrocers, farm shops, markets and specialist ethnic grocers.

ORGANIC

TIPS FOR CHOOSING THE FRUIT/VEGETABLE

- Pick fresh – never frozen, dried, cooked or treated in any way.
- If possible, buy organic, as these are much less likely to have been sprayed with chemicals that may cause problems with germination.
- Obviously, seedless varieties won't have any pips in, so avoid those. Unfortunately this includes all varieties of bananas sold in the shops.
- Ideally, choose fruits of a named variety. In supermarkets, all fruit and vegetables should be labelled with their variety name. In smaller shops, don't be afraid to ask the proprietor what variety something is.

RIPENING UP

Having obtained the fruit or vegetable, it is crucial that it is ripe before you extract the pips. Success is more likely with something that is bought when it is in season, but it is not essential if it is properly ripened. Many fruits and vegetables are sold under-ripe in the shops, and will need ripening at home before the pips can be used. Placing the pip fruit near ripe bananas and in a warm, sunny spot will speed up the ripening process.

HARVESTING PIPS

Once extracted, wash off the pips thoroughly, making sure they are completely clean. Some pips will need further treatments (see the individual pip growing pages). Then plant them as soon as possible.

SMALLER PIPS CAN BE WASHED UNDER THE TAP IN A SIEVE

LARGER PIPS WILL NEED TO BE SCRUBBED

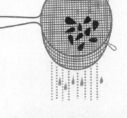

Putting the pips between some moist kitchen towel or in a sealed plastic bag will prevent them drying out if they have to be left for a couple of days, but try not to delay longer than that.

WHAT PLANTS NEED TO GROW WELL

Everything in the food chain depends on the ability of plants to make their own food. Plants do this through a process called photosynthesis, meaning 'making from light' (from the Greek 'photo', light, and 'synthesis', to make). The sugars created by photosynthesis are used as energy to fuel other processes, in a constant cycle of creation that allows the plant to grow.

PHOTOSYNTHESIS

Plants absorb the energy from sunlight into their cells through a chemical called chlorophyll that occurs in all the green parts of the plant.

Carbon dioxide is taken into the leaves through tiny holes in the leaf surface that can open and close depending on the plants' needs, the time of day and the weather conditions.

LIGHT + WATER + CARBON DIOXIDE = GLUCOSE + OXYGEN

Using the energy from sunlight, plants turn water and carbon dioxide into sugars (glucose), which are then converted into carbohydrates such as starch.

Water is absorbed from the soil by the roots and transported up the stem or trunk to the leaves.

GETTING IT RIGHT

To get plants to grow well, it is important to get the essentials right: light, water, air for carbon dioxide, and nutrients. Too little of one, even with surplus of the others, will lead to limited growth of the plant.

When growing plants indoors, light can often be the most difficult thing to supply. The quality and duration of daylight depends on the aspect of the windows. Many plants originating in sunny countries will not thrive on a gloomy windowsill. Likewise, plants used to growing in shady forests won't appreciate direct sunlight.

Always give the pip plants the best spot possible, but remember to rotate the pot regularly to ensure even growth; otherwise, the leaves and stems will all grow towards the light, creating a lopsided plant.

Older plants will accumulate dust on their leaves. It is important to clean them regularly by giving them a blast with the shower, or wiping each one off individually. This ensures the light can get straight into the leaf, and that the tiny air holes will not get blocked.

Watering and feeding (supplying nutrients) are covered on pages 44–49.

WHERE TO GROW THE PIPS

INDOORS

In the absence of a greenhouse or conservatory, windowsills are the best spot for pots of pips. Check the requirements of each one as to how much sun it likes – south- and west-facing will be the best for sun-lovers; those that don't mind less light will do well on east- and north-facing windowsills.

However, check that the plants are not sitting in a draught, especially if the windows are not double-glazed. A cold draught will do more damage than the light will do good. All the pips will do well at room temperature (18–20°C).

In warmer weather, it is also important to make sure the leaves don't get too hot and scorch, so be prepared to move the pots further away from the window. In summer, if it is not too cold at night, many plants will appreciate being outdoors for a month or two anyway. Check if they are hardy enough in the growing information for each pip.

OUTDOORS

Siting pots outside follows the same principles as inside. Give the plants as much light as possible (if they want it), and put them in a sheltered rather than a windy spot.

Convenience also comes into play here – plants that are grown near the house are more easily monitored, watered and cared for than those at the end of the garden, so keep them on a patio or around a door if possible.

The same applies to growing pips in the ground. Older plants can be moved to the backs of borders, but seedlings need more attention, so plant them in a bed that can be tended from the path and that gets enough light and rain falling on it. Be wary of beds alongside buildings and fences as they are often in a 'rain shadow' (shielded from the rain by the height of the walls), so the soil is generally very dry.

BASIC EQUIPMENT

Growing pips does not require a large range of specialist apparatus, or indeed any actual gardening tools at all. Almost everything needed can be found in the average kitchen and household, and the rest is easily and cheaply available. Different pips will require slightly different equipment, but these are the basics.

Pots or trays to grow the pips in, from small to large, depending on the pip size and how big it grows.

Saucers or trays to put the pots on so they don't leave stains on the surfaces where they are placed.

Compost for growing in pots: widely available in small to large bags in supermarkets, garden centres and other household stores.

A trowel or other form of scoop (even a big spoon) to transfer compost from the bag to your pot.

A sharp knife and/or metal skewer to pierce the outer shell of some pips.

A sieve and piece of muslin cloth to line it for cleaning smaller pips. A coffee filter paper could work instead of the muslin.

Clear plastic covers or clingfilm for trays, and/or clear plastic bags (food bags are good) to cover pots, and elastic bands to fasten the bags over the pots.

Labels and a pencil or waterproof **pen** to add the name and date of the pips sown.

A watering can or similar water receptacle, such as a plastic bottle.

A spray/misting bottle, useful for cleaning leaves and maintaining humidity around the plant if necessary. Ensure old cosmetics bottles are completely clean first.

A dibber – a pencil or teaspoon are excellent substitutes – to help ease small seedlings and plants out of their pots and trays into new ones.

A pair of secateurs or sharp scissors to cut back plants.

A spade and a **rake** for preparing the soil and planting pips outside. **A trowel** and **hand fork** are useful for planting small, young plants.

WHAT TO GROW PIPS IN INDOORS

POTS, TRAYS AND COMPOST

It is easy to get carried away when faced with the wide range of equipment available to buy in garden centres, but there are only a few essential items.

Pots

No matter what the pot is made of, make sure it has drainage holes in the bottom. Small pots are best to start pips off in; they can then be transferred to larger ones as they grow.

Plastic is cheapest and comes in standard sizes: 9cm (the diameter of the top), then 1 litre (capacity), 1.5l, 2l, 5l, and so on.

Terracotta or ceramic pots are more attractive, but also more expensive. Pots made from coir or reinforced cardboard are often sold for starting off seedlings, and these are also suitable for sowing pips in. As they are biodegradable, the whole thing, plant and pot, can be then planted into the next size up without disturbing the roots.

It is also possible to buy pot-specific saucers in both terracotta and plastic. Saucers are useful for protecting windowsills against water that flows through the compost and out of the pot. Pots can also be watered by filling up the saucer with water that is then absorbed up through the compost, thus avoiding splashing/disturbing the plant/seedlings with water.

Trays

For sowing a lot of small pips at once, a tray can be better than a pot. Seed trays are made from sturdy plastic and have drainage holes in their base. Pips sown in these can get their roots all tangled together, but there's plenty of surface space to sow a lot of pips at once.

Alternatively, sow one or two pips in each cell of a modular insert (a plastic tray divided into smaller spaces). These are flimsier, and are best contained within a seed tray. Choose a smaller number of cells (e.g. 24). Inserts with more cells will need watering more often and it will be less time before the plants outgrow them.

To create a mini-greenhouse, it is also possible to buy a clear plastic cover to fit over the seed tray, which will raise the temperature and humidity around the seedlings – good for tropical plants.

Heated propagators

Although it is not essential, most pips will germinate faster with a bit of extra heat underneath them, and this can be supplied using a heated propagator. This is a tray and cover as above, but with an electrically heated mat in the base, on to which pots can be placed to keep warm.

Compost

For starting off pips indoors, choose a proprietary seedling or potting-on compost as it is a finer grade and won't contain chunks of woodchip that would clog up a small pot or tray. Some plants require a specifically acidic compost known as 'ericaceous', which is sometimes also sold as 'Rhododendron and Camellia compost'. In general, the price of compost reflects its quality, so if possible choose the most expensive one.

RECYCLED CONTAINERS

As well as supplying the pips, the kitchen is a good source of containers to grow them in. This saves the expense of buying pots or trays, especially for the first one or two pips.

Things to consider

Make sure the container is completely clean before using it – rotting food could spread disease to the growing pip.

Choose an appropriate size for the pip and the stage of growth it is at: don't swamp a tiny plant in a big pot or squeeze a big plant into a tiny one. Small yoghurt pots are ideal for starting individual small pips such as lemon or apple. For sowing lots of smaller pips at once, such as passion fruit, plastic mushroom trays are good. Larger pips or plants being potted on can go into big yoghurt or ice-cream pots or food cans. The pip-growing information gives an indication of the size needed using the standard pot measurements, so use this as a guide.

Use a container of a material that is not going to disintegrate through regular watering. Plastic is best, but for pips that won't take long to germinate (check the icons for each pip for details), thicker cardboard such as toilet-roll tubes can suffice.

Don't use metal containers for pips that will either be in direct contact with heat (e.g. on a radiator) or in direct sunlight. At the very least, they will need more frequent watering as the heat causes the soil to dry out faster, and they may even get hot enough to dry out the roots themselves.

HOW TO MAKE DRAINAGE HOLES

Whatever the size of the container, it must have drainage holes in the bottom. It may be necessary to make these.

1 Taking appropriate safety precautions, use a metal skewer, knife or scissors for plastic pots.

2 Metal cans are best pierced using a sharp nail hammered through the base and then removed. Four or five holes are sufficient for each pot – the smaller the pot, the smaller each hole needs to be.

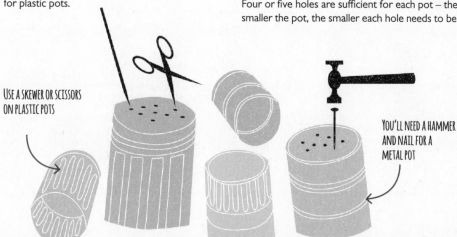

USE A SKEWER OR SCISSORS ON PLASTIC POTS

YOU'LL NEED A HAMMER AND NAIL FOR A METAL POT

WHAT TO GROW PIPS IN OUTDOORS

Some of the pips, such as the tree fruit and vegetables, can be planted outdoors. Others need to be started off indoors but can be moved in the summer into a bigger pot outdoors once they have grown into a small plant. Check each pip's growing information for whether it can be grown outside or not.

POTS AND COMPOST

It is possible to be just as imaginative with the containers for growing pips in outdoors as it is indoors. If the container has drainage holes, or can have drainage holes made in it, it is suitable – why not try growing in an old pair of boots, or a wooden crate? Containers without drainage holes, such as old teapots, can be used but it's much easier to overwater the plants within them. Take extra care to monitor the soil and check the moisture levels as deep as you can within the container before watering.

Standard pots are usually plastic or terracotta. Choose a suitable size for your pip, but remember that the compost in small pots will dry out faster and that they will be more prone to being blown over in windy weather. If you don't have a garden it needn't limit the possibilities for growing pips outdoors – a windowbox will do just as well.

Any proprietary multi-purpose compost is fine for filling larger pots. The plants going in them are bigger, and their roots more robust, so they no longer need the fine-grade composts used for younger plants.

Any plant grown in a pot will need occasional repotting every one to three years, as this refreshes the compost and the nutrients therein (see page 116).

A well-rooted plant will be very difficult to remove from a pot that is narrower at the top than in the middle, so don't leave one in there for too long.

THE GROUND

Although all of the pips will benefit from the extra protection they gain from being sown and raised initially in a pot, some of them (pumpkins and apple trees, for example) can be grown into larger plants outside in the ground.

PREPARING THE GROUND

It is important to prepare the ground before planting anything into it, by following these steps:

1 Dig over the area thoroughly, turning the soil over to at least the depth of the spade and breaking up any large clumps.

2 Remove all weeds as you dig, getting out the roots as well as the green tops.

3 Take out any large stones or rubble. Smaller stones and gravel can be left in the soil; they will aid drainage.

4 Spread a layer of compost over the area. This could be bought or homemade, or could be any other form of well-rotted matter such as horse manure or spent mushroom compost. As long as it is brown and crumbly it is ready to use. Use a garden fork or spade to mix it in with the soil.

5 The soil level will by now be higher than it was originally, so lightly tread down the large air pockets, then rake it level.

SOIL TYPES

If the soil is quite sandy (i.e. it is fine and crumbles easily like sand), mix in plenty of well-rotted compost to add nutrients and help it to retain water.

If the soil is more like clay (i.e. sticky when wet and breaks only into larger clods), compost that is not quite rotted down, or horse manure with a bit of straw still in it (but not fresh), will help break up the consistency and aid water drainage. Just make sure the soil surface is raked smooth and doesn't have any lumpy compost bits on it that might impede the growth of the young plants.

Even the poorest soil can be transformed over the years by the regular addition of compost or other well-rotted matter.

SOWING THE PIPS

Instructions on sowing the pips are listed under each pip project, but all follow a few basic ground rules:

Ideally most of the pips would be sown in the spring, but they can be sown all year round as long as they get enough heat and light.

Make sure your pot or tray is the right size for your pip, is clean and has drainage holes.

Once you have filled a pot or tray with compost, tap it down on the work surface a couple of times to shake out any air gaps, and use an empty pot or tray on the top to press the compost down gently. Make sure the surface is level and leave a lip of about a centimetre at the top so the compost doesn't wash over the sides when it is being watered.

Always water the compost so that it is moist all the way through before sowing the pips; if you do it after sowing, the pips might get sluiced to one side of the pot/tray.

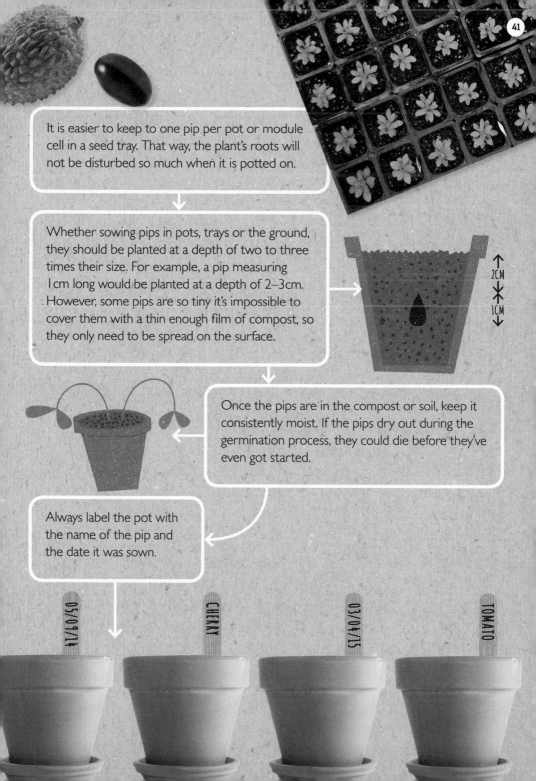

It is easier to keep to one pip per pot or module cell in a seed tray. That way, the plant's roots will not be disturbed so much when it is potted on.

Whether sowing pips in pots, trays or the ground, they should be planted at a depth of two to three times their size. For example, a pip measuring 1cm long would be planted at a depth of 2–3cm. However, some pips are so tiny it's impossible to cover them with a thin enough film of compost, so they only need to be spread on the surface.

2CM
1CM

Once the pips are in the compost or soil, keep it consistently moist. If the pips dry out during the germination process, they could die before they've even got started.

Always label the pot with the name of the pip and the date it was sown.

05/09/14

CHERRY

03/04/15

TOMATO

SPECIAL TREATMENT

Some pips will need special treatment before or after they are sown. These processes have been developed by gardeners to mimic what would happen to the pip in the wild in order to break the pip's dormancy and get it to germinate successfully.

A fake winter

The seeds and pips of many plants are dispersed in the autumn, but if they were to germinate then they would be promptly killed off by the cold and wet of winter. They have therefore evolved to sit tight in the soil until spring, when the weather warms up and the light levels increase. Putting the pips in the fridge for a few weeks fools them into thinking that months of winter have passed, and they germinate once they are taken out and sown in a warm place.

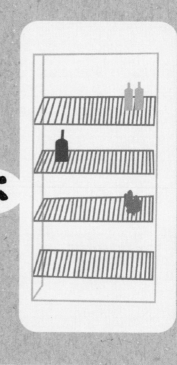

TESTING SEEDS ARE VIABLE

To save wasting time sowing bad pips, check that they are viable first. Examine them carefully – are they undamaged? Do they feel solid? A good, quick test to indicate the probable viability of many pips is to put them in a glass of water. Viable pips generally sink to the bottom, empty pips that have not developed properly (and therefore won't germinate) float.

Breaking the shell

Other pips have a very hard outer shell to protect them from damage and to ensure they only start to absorb water and germinate when the circumstances are just right. Sometimes this shell is broken down by the stomach acid of the creatures that eat the fruit; other times it is degraded by prolonged soaking in water, or by physical damage to the pip from animals or the elements.

All of these processes can be mimicked. Soaking the pip in water is straightforward; otherwise the shell can be rubbed with sandpaper or nicked with a sharp knife to allow water to enter the pip.

Turn up the heat

Pips from warm climates are used to germinating in soil that has a higher temperature than the average soil or pot of compost indoors, especially if the pips are being sown in the colder months.

This can be combated by sowing the pips in pots indoors and placing the pots over a heat source. This is best supplied by a heated propagator system, which can be thermostatically controlled, but putting the pot on a saucer and then on top of a radiator can do the trick as well.

WATERING

All plants grown in pots inside need regular watering – and rain is usually not enough to keep pots outside adequately moist. Pips and plants grown in the ground need less attention, but still can have insufficient root systems to find water in dry weather, so may also need periodic watering.

As plants can't tell you when they need water, the first indication can be drooping leaves and stems. However, by the time the leaves start to wilt the plant will have been suffering for a while. It definitely won't have been growing properly, and may also be at a higher risk of succumbing to pests and diseases. It is best to check every day if they need watering, and the easiest method is to assess the soil.

CHECKING IF YOUR PLANT NEEDS WATER

Plants like the soil to be not too wet and not too dry: if it is moist all the way through the pot it is just right. Check the soil by sticking a finger into the pot near the edge (so as not to damage the roots too much).

If it is too wet, the soil will be squishy, dark in colour and little puddles might form where the soil has been compressed – it doesn't need water today.

If it is too dry the soil will be crumbly, light in colour, and dry to the touch. It needs water now!

When it is just right, it will feel slightly damp and a bit of soil will stick to the skin. It doesn't need water today, but remember to check again tomorrow.

WATERING CANS AND DEVICES

Watering cans come in all shapes and sizes. Small ones are best for small pots, so that the soil doesn't get washed over the side when it is being watered. Using a spout with a rose (a flat end with lots of smaller holes) also helps prevent this. It is also possible to make a watering device by buying bottle top waterers – tiny spouts that screw on to the top of a normal drink bottle. These are good for very small plants, when the pips are just starting to grow.

HOW TO WATER YOUR PLANT

Pour the water on gently to avoid washing away the soil and damaging the roots. Always water the soil, not the plant's leaves, by getting the spout of the can as close to the soil surface as possible. Watering the leaves wastes water as not much will make it to the soil; it also increases the likelihood of fungal diseases taking hold on larger plants.

With small plants and seedlings it is inevitable that the leaves will get wet, but providing there is plenty of air circulation it shouldn't be a problem. They will also bounce back to growing upright if the weight of the water has toppled them over, but giving them a hand by gently pulling them back up — by holding a leaf, never the delicate stem — will help.

Continue watering until water starts to come out of the bottom of the pot. It is best to keep the pot on a saucer to prevent it making a mess.

If the plant has got really dry, it will need watering again an hour or two later to make sure the water really sinks into the soil.

An alternative is to put the pot into the sink or a tray of water and leave it to soak up through the bottom. This takes a few hours. Once the soil is moist all the way to the surface, take the pot out.

Never leave a potted plant constantly sitting in water, as the roots will drown.

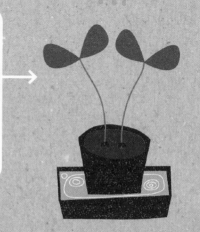

FEEDING

All pips contain the energy and nutrients they need to break free of their shells and start growing roots and leaves, but after that they rely on what they are growing in to supply their water and nutrients.

THE BASICS

Soil and compost, bought or homemade, contain a basic level of nutrition. In proprietary seedling, potting and multi-purpose composts these will be in measured proportions for balanced growth, but limited quantities. Most composts will have enough nutrients in them to last 3–6 months – check the packaging to be sure.

ADDED NUTRIENTS

Whatever the plant is growing in, including the ground outside, it will need extra fertiliser (food) after a while. This can be in granular, controlled-release (often called 'slow-release') form, which is mixed in with the compost at planting time, or liquid form, which is added to the water of the growing plant. Liquid fertilisers get into the plant faster, and are good for a quick boost to growth or correcting a nutrient deficiency.

Different fertilisers contain different levels of each nutrient. Those labelled for flowering and fruiting (rose and tomato feeds, for example), will be high in potassium to promote just that, and don't have much in them for producing healthy leaves and roots. A balanced fertiliser will be best for the pips. These will have a roughly equal ratio of nitrogen (N) to phosphorus (P) to potassium (K), so look for the N:P:K ratio on the label.

FOLLOW THE INSTRUCTIONS

It can be tempting to pile on the fertiliser to get bigger and better plants more quickly, but overfeeding will result in the nutrients reaching toxic levels in the soil, which could potentially kill the plant. Follow the instructions on the packet for the appropriate dose and frequency.

POTASSIUM

CHAPTER 3
THE PIPS

This chapter covers all the details of how to grow a wide range of pips. From the exotic papaya and dragon fruit to the more usual tomatoes and raspberries, there is a project for everyone. Don't be put off growing exotic fruits – many are faster and easier to grow than the less exotic.

At the top of each pip project are two series of icons. The first rates the easiness of the project: one is the easiest, three is a bit more involved. The second series rates how much patience will be needed to grow the pips: one is for those that grow quickly, three is for pips that can grow into trees and take more time before they do anything. The ultimate size of the plant and where it will be happy growing is easily seen in the 'Stats'. An ideal sowing time is specified for each pip, but they can be sown all year round, provided they are given enough light and heat.

All of the pip plants can be further multiplied by taking cuttings. Those with the highest potential success rates are indicated under 'Care of the Plant'.

AVOCADO
Persea americana

EASINESS: 🌢🌢 **PATIENCE:** 🌢🌢 **TYPE:** TREE; PERENNIAL

Avocados are one of the most spectacular pips to grow: it's amazing to see the roots and shoot break the pip open down the middle. You'd have to grow it into a large tree to even stand a chance of picking avocados from it, but it makes a pretty plant for the windowsill. In method 1, the pip is grown in water to start with, so it's possible to watch both the roots and shoot develop. Method 2 is easier, and also avoids the fiddly process of transplanting the rooted pip. Ideally, sow the pips in April but any time of year is possible.

EQUIPMENT
- Avocado
- 3 cocktail sticks
- Glass tumbler or small bowl
- Small (9cm) pot of compost (later)

STATS
SOW: INDOORS
GROW: INDOORS
MINIMUM
TEMPERATURE: 20°C
FULL HEIGHT: 2M

METHOD 1

❶ Start by cleaning any avocado flesh off the pip. Soaking it for 48 hours in tepid water will make the sides easy to pierce and give it a good head start.

❷ Take your pip with the pointy end upward. Use a cocktail stick to pierce the pip's side, roughly in the middle of the pip. Repeat with another two cocktail sticks around the circumference.

❸ Fill a glass or small bowl almost to the top with water, then carefully balance the pip on its sticks over the top. The bottom half of the pip should be submerged in the water. Put it all in a warm, sunny spot and change the water every couple of days.

❹ Germination will take a few weeks. The roots will start to grow out of the bottom of the pip, then a shoot will appear from the top. Once the shoot has four leaves, very carefully take the pip out of the glass, remove the cocktail sticks, and plant it into a small pot of pre-watered compost.

AVOCADO
Continued

METHOD 2

1 Clean and soak the pip as in Method 1.

2 Plant the pip into the pre-watered compost, with the pointed end upwards, so that half of the pip is submerged in the compost and the rest remains sticking out of the soil.

3 Put the whole pot into a clear plastic bag and fasten it at the top. Keep the pot somewhere warm – if possible, provide some heat underneath it by putting it on a saucer on a radiator or in a heated propagator (without the bag). Check it every couple of days to ensure the compost is still moist, and water if necessary.

4 Germination will take a few weeks. The first signs of growth may be the root coming out of the bottom of the pot. Once the shoot is visible, remove the bag.

CARE OF THE PLANT

1 Keep the plant in a bright spot (direct sunlight is not necessary) in a warm room (20°C) at all times. Pot on as necessary, finishing with as large a pot as there is space for.

2 Avocados grow quite tall and leggy, and won't branch naturally for about a year. Support the stem with a small cane. To make a bushier plant, once the shoot has grown about 10 leaves, cut off the very tip and top leaf from the stem. This will make the plant produce offshoots to the side.

EQUIPMENT

- Equipment
- Avocado
- Small (9cm) pot of compost
- Plastic bag and tie

MELON AND WATERMELON
Cucumis melo and *Citrullus lanatus*

EASINESS: 🌢 **PATIENCE:** 🌢 **TYPE:** TRAILING/CLIMBER; ANNUAL

Melons and watermelons contain ample pips. If they can be provided with the long period of warm weather they require to fruit successfully, the trailing vines may produce their own (water)melons, but they may not taste as good as the original. Ideally, sow the pips in April but any time of year is possible.

EQUIPMENT

- Melon or watermelon
- Sieve
- Small (9cm) pot(s) or a seed tray with modular insert
- Compost
- Canes or other stakes and twine for support if growing upwards

METHOD

❶ Melons and watermelons are ripe when they smell sweet and sound hollow when knocked. Keep the fruit a day or two beyond this point before cutting them open and scooping out the pips.

❷ Wash the pips in a sieve – use a little washing up liquid to remove the sugars – then sow individually in small pots or the cells of a modular seed tray. The seedlings dislike their roots being disturbed, so this will minimise that effect when repotting. Keep the pots/tray at a minimum of 16°C. Germination will take 1–2 weeks.

CARE OF THE PLANT

❶ Keep the plants in a sunny, warm spot, repotting into a medium then a large (7.5l) pot. To fruit they will need many weeks in daytime temperatures of at least 25°C, constant moisture and regular feeding.

❷ Once the seedling has at least three pairs of leaves, take out the tip and the top pair to encourage side shoots. Take out the tips of these as well, and the subsequent side shoots from those branches, to form eight stems.

❸ Tie the stems to supports if space is limited, and provide support for any growing fruit. An old pair of tights or other underwear is surprisingly effective for this.

STATS
SOW: INDOORS
GROW: INDOORS
MINIMUM
TEMPERATURE: 16°C
FULL HEIGHT: 2M

CITRUS
Citrus species

EASINESS: ● **PATIENCE:** ●● **TYPE:** TREE; PERENNIAL

Citrus trees, with their glossy evergreen foliage and strongly scented blossoms, make fantastic houseplants or plants for the patio. Ideally, sow the pips in April but any time of year is possible.

EQUIPMENT
- Citrus (lemon, orange, lime, grapefruit, etc.)
- Small (9cm) pots or seed tray with modular insert
- Compost
- Plastic bag or cover for seed tray

METHOD

1 Extract and wash the pips, taking care to only use whole ones if the fruit was cut across the middle. Sow the pips singly in the module insert, or space well apart in the pot/tray. Some citrus pips have the unusual quality of what's known as being polyembryonic: that is, they will produce more than one shoot/plant from a single seed. At least one of these seedlings will be genetically identical to the parent. Unfortunately, there is no way to tell which is which until they fruit (which can take up to 6 years), but it's worth keeping all the plants anyway. Sowing the pips singly ensures it's possible to tell if any of them are polyembryonic.

2 Put the pot in a bag and seal the top, or cover the seed tray. Keep the compost consistently moist and the pots/trays at 16–21°C. Germination should take 2–8 weeks.

3 Once the first shoots have appeared, remove the bag or cover and keep in a warm place to grow on. Any polyembryonic seedlings will need to be carefully separated and planted in their own pots once they have at least four leaves.

STATS

SOW: INDOORS
GROW: INDOORS/OUTDOORS
MINIMUM
TEMPERATURE: 6°C
FULL HEIGHT: 1—2M

CITRUS
Continued

CARE OF THE PLANT

① Citrus trees like a lot of light, so keep them in the sunniest spot possible, and clean the leaves regularly. They will also prefer to be outdoors over the summer, but bring them indoors or protect them with fleece in the winter: they should be protected from frosts, cold winds/ draughts and ideally not be kept below 6°C. Should the plant start to flower, it will need a minimum of 14°C for about 6 months to produce fruit.

② Keep repotting the plants as they need it, finishing with as large a pot as there is space for. The plants will also prefer it if their compost is allowed to almost dry out between waterings, rather than being kept moist all the time. If a plant starts to fruit, don't let it dry out completely as this may cause the fruit to fall off.

③ Citrus trees are naturally branching, and will need little pruning to encourage a good shape. They are slow-growing, putting on around 30cm a year, depending on the size of the pot and level of feeding provided, but can ultimately get quite big, so may need pruning in later life to control their size.

④ For a more striking plant, train it into a standard – a lollipop shape of a clear stem of 50–75cm with a bush of foliage on top. Guide the seedling up a cane until it reaches the desired height. Leave side branches on for the first 2 years, but then remove them, leaving only the ones at the top, and continue to remove side shoots off the stem. The stem will need supporting for several years until it can take the weight of the foliage on top. Citrus trees are suitable for cuttings (see pages 136–7).

PASSION FRUIT
Passiflora edulis

EASINESS: 🌢 **PATIENCE:** 🌢🌢 **TYPE:** CLIMBER; PERENNIAL

Passion flowers make beautiful climbers, with lush, twining foliage and showy flowers. Some varieties grow happily outdoors, but the type that produces edible fruit needs a frost-free environment. They can be restricted to make them suitable for growing indoors, but require a larger space to grow into mature plants. Ideally, sow the pips in April but any time of year is possible.

EQUIPMENT
- Passion fruit
- A small bowl or Tupperware pot
- Sieve
- Kitchen towel
- Small (9cm) pot of compost

STATS
SOW: INDOORS
GROW: INDOORS
MINIMUM
TEMPERATURE: 10°C
FULL HEIGHT: 6M

METHOD

❶ Passion fruit pips need to be allowed to ferment in the fruit juices to make them more likely to germinate. The easiest way to do this is to keep the fruit until it has shrivelled up to half its original size, but is still moist inside (buying more than one fruit allows for testing this without cutting open the final fruit).

❷ The pips then need extracting from the little juice sacs that surround them. Squeeze them out on to some kitchen towel, which prevents too much mess from squirting juice, wash in a sieve and leave to dry on a plate.

❸ Alternatively, cut open the ripe fruit and scoop out the flesh and pips into a small bowl or Tupperware pot. Leave this (covered: it will smell), in a warm place for a few days to allow the pips to ferment.

❹ Carefully pour off the very top of the mould, leaving most of the pips still in the bowl. Tip these into a sieve and push around under running water to remove the juice sacs, then dry on a plate so they are easier to handle.

❺ Sow the pips once they are dry (they won't store well), in pots of pre-watered compost. Keep at 20–25°C and they should germinate within 2–4 weeks.

CARE OF THE PLANT

❶ Transplant the seedlings once they have reached 20–30cm tall, and give the stems the support of canes, a wigwam or wires to grow up. The plant's final pot should be no smaller than 35 cm in diameter.

❷ Passion fruit plants can be pruned back to a framework after flowering. Cut back all the side shoots, leaving a branch of two leaves long from the main stem. The main stems can also be shortened by a third.

❸ The plant is suitable to take cuttings from in spring to late summer (see pages 136–7).

LYCHEE
Litchi chinensis

EASINESS: 🌢 **PATIENCE:** 🌢 **TYPE:** TREE; PERENNIAL

The lychee fruit produces an evergreen tree with young foliage in shades of orange and red. It makes a good houseplant but only for a few years, until it gets too big. Ideally, sow the pips in March but any time of year is possible.

EQUIPMENT
- Lychee
- Small (9cm) pot(s)
- Compost – ericaceous is best

METHOD
❶ When the lychee has turned a dull brown colour, score carefully around the fruit – from top to tail – and peel back the skin and flesh to reveal the shiny pip. Remove and wash it. It must be sown within a couple of days, preferably immediately, or it will lose its viability.

❷ Plant in a pot of pre-watered compost and keep at 21°C until germinated, making sure the compost does not dry out. Germination should take around 2–3 weeks.

❸ Once the shoots appear, ensure the seedlings are not in direct sunlight.

CARE OF THE PLANT
❶ Repot as necessary, continuing to use ericaceous compost, mixed with a little grit if possible to make it more free-draining. The plant will be happy at room temperature, in an open, sunny position.

❷ The plant's growth will slow in the winter, and it will need less water at this time. Lychee plants like slightly acidic soil, so ericaceous compost is best. Watering with tap water will make the compost more alkaline; if possible, use rainwater, which is more acidic.

❸ Keep the plant for as long as it fits in its space (it will take about 3 years to get to 2m) rather than pruning it.

STATS
SOW: INDOORS
GROW: INDOORS
MINIMUM
TEMPERATURE: 15°C
FULL HEIGHT: 2M

CAPE GOOSEBERRY
Physalis peruvians

EASINESS: ◖ **PATIENCE:** ◖ **TYPE:** BUSH; PERENNIAL

The golden fruits of the cape gooseberry, in their little papery lantern shades, are borne prolifically on the shrubby plants. Although a perennial, they are often grown outdoors as an annual crop instead, fruiting in late summer and autumn. Pips sown should produce plants that will bear fruit that year. Ideally, sow the pips in March but any time of year is possible.

EQUIPMENT
- Cape gooseberry
- Small bowl and a wooden spoon
- OR a sieve and piece of (muslin) cloth
- Small (9cm) pot of compost
- Plastic bag and tie

STATS
SOW: INDOORS
GROW: INDOORS/OUTDOORS
MINIMUM
TEMPERATURE: 1°C
FULL HEIGHT: 1.2M

METHOD

❶ There are two methods to extract the many seeds from the flesh of the cape gooseberry. Start by removing the outer casings around the fruit.

❷ Either put the fruit(s) in a small bowl and mash carefully with a wooden spoon. Add water to the bowl and leave it for an hour or two. The flesh will float to the top, and the pips sink to the bottom. Carefully pour off the water and flesh to leave the pips.

❸ Alternatively, cut the fruit in half and squash through a sieve lined with a piece of muslin (the pips are small enough to go through just the sieve). It helps to do this under running water.

❹ Remove the pips from the bowl or muslin and dry on a plate to make them easier to handle. Sow in the pot of pre-watered compost, only just covering the pips as they prefer a bit of light to germinate. Put the pot in a plastic bag and tie up the top to help keep the compost moist.

❺ The pips will germinate within 2–3 weeks when kept in a warm place (15–18°C), so check every day for signs of shoots and remove the bag when they appear.

CARE OF THE PLANT

❶ Once the seedlings have about five leaves they can be repotted, and then repotted again or planted into the garden; support them with stakes or canes. Only put them outside once there is no more risk of a frost, and keep them in a sunny spot. The tips of the plants can be pinched out to create a bushier plant if desired.

PAPAYA
Carica papaya

EASINESS: ◗ **PATIENCE:** ◗   **TYPE:** BUSH/TREE; PERENNIAL

Papayas have a high pip yield. The plant looks something like a palm tree, with a tall fleshy stem and a crop of leaves on top. They are fast-growing too, so are perhaps best grown just as a novelty plant for a single season. Ideally, sow the pips in April but any time of year is possible.

EQUIPMENT
- Papaya
- Kitchen towel
- Sieve
- Small (9cm) pot of compost
- Plastic bag and tie

STATS
SOW: INDOORS
GROW: INDOORS
MINIMUM
TEMPERATURE: 13°C
FULL HEIGHT: 3.5M

METHOD 1

1 Cut the papaya open and scoop out some of the pips on to a piece of kitchen towel. Press down on each one individually, piercing the sac of juice with a fingernail to reveal the corrugated pip. Wash the pips in a sieve. They can be kept for a few days in the fridge between some moist kitchen towel or sown straight away.

2 Sow the pips in a pot of pre-watered compost, then put the whole pot in a plastic bag and seal the top. Put it on a saucer on a radiator or in a heated propagator (minus the bag) – the pips need a temperature of 24–30°C to germinate.

3 Remove the bag when shoots appear (within 2–4 weeks). The seedlings will grow quickly; they like plenty of sunlight and warmth but do not need the high temperatures they require to germinate. They are prone to fungal infections, so take care when watering not to get any water on the leaves.

CARE OF THE PLANT

1 Repot the seedlings straight into their final pot – as large as you want to allow the plant to get – as they do not like disturbance. Keep them in a warm spot in bright sunlight and moist compost and feed them well. They will not need pruning.

MANGO
Mangifera indica

EASINESS: 🌢🌢 **PATIENCE:** 🌢🌢🌢 **TYPE:** TREE; PERENNIAL

The mango pip is quite complicated to deal with. However, it likes being grown in a pot, and its attractive young stems grow through red to pink to copper before turning green. Ideally, sow the pips in March but any time of year is possible.

EQUIPMENT

- Mango
- Sharp knife
- Wire wool or wire dish scrubber
- Scissors (optional, see Method 2)
- Jam jar or glass
- Medium (1l) pot of compost
- Plastic bag and tie

METHOD 1

1 Remove the pip from the fruit and wash, scrape and scrub off the pulp – the husk will still be hairy. There are now two options – to plant the whole husk, or to open it to reveal the actual pip and plant that (see Method 2).

2 If leaving the pip in the husk, make a nick in the husk on the edge of the flatter end to allow water to penetrate. Put the whole thing in a jar or glass of water and keep it at 21°C for 2 weeks (an airing cupboard is ideal). Change the water daily. Remove from the jar and plant. If it hasn't already produced a shoot, seal the pot in a plastic bag until it does.

STATS
SOW: INDOORS
GROW: INDOORS
MINIMUM
TEMPERATURE: 20°C
FULL HEIGHT: 2M

MANGO
Continued

METHOD 2

1 Alternatively, to extract the pip, leave the cleaned husk to dry overnight. Using a strong pair of scissors, clip out a triangle shape from the edge at the flatter end, big enough to allow the point of a knife to be inserted. Work the knife into the husk carefully to pry the two sides apart without damaging the pip inside. Push the pip into a pot of pre-watered compost and seal in the bag.

2 Keep the bagged pot at 21°C until a shoot appears (this could take up to 2 months, so check regularly that the compost is still moist), and then transfer to a bright spot. The seedlings do not like direct sunlight, and will also need acclimatising to the drier atmosphere outside the bag. Remove the bag for only a few hours at first, gradually increasing the time the seedlings are in the open air.

CARE OF THE PLANT

1 Repot the plant as necessary and then annually when it's in its final pot. They prefer acidic conditions, so use ericaceous compost if possible. Keep in a bright, warm spot out of direct sunlight. Mangos appreciate a high-potassium feed in the summer, but require less watering in the winter.

2 Prune to encourage a bushy shape: take the top bud/leaves out once it's a year old, and continue to take out the tips of stems as necessary to promote branching and restrict its size.

KIWI
Actinidia deliciosa

EASINESS: **PATIENCE:** **TYPE:** CLIMBER; PERENNIAL

The kiwi plant is a decorative climber, and will happily romp over a fence, wall or trellis in the garden. Alternatively, grow it on a wigwam in a pot indoors, but it will need pruning, otherwise it will get too big to be a houseplant. Ideally, sow the pips in March but any time of year is possible.

EQUIPMENT
- Kiwi
- Sieve
- Small (9cm) pot of compost
- Plastic bag and tie

STATS
SOW: INDOORS
GROW: INDOORS/OUTDOORS
MINIMUM
TEMPERATURE: −8°C
FULL HEIGHT: 2M+

METHOD

1 Scoop out some of the pips into the sieve and wash off the flesh. If they are not to be sown immediately, dry them on a plate and store in a plastic bag or pot in the fridge.

2 Sow in a pot of pre-watered compost, then put the whole pot in a plastic bag and seal the top. Keep in a warm spot – a sunny windowsill at room temperature is sufficient – and check daily to ensure the compost has not dried out. Water it if necessary until shoots appear, when the bag should be removed. Germination takes a few weeks. If nothing is happening, try giving the pot a mock winter by putting it in the fridge for a month, then returning it to the windowsill.

3 The seedlings will be happy growing on the sunny windowsill until they need repotting (when they get to around 5cm tall).

CARE OF THE PLANT

1 Repot as necessary, and give the plant supports (canes, a wigwam or wires) to grow up. It will be happy in sun or partial shade (indoors or out). If transplanting to the garden to grow against a wall or fence, prepare the wires for it to scramble over first, and plant out once the plant has reached around 30cm tall, hardening off as necessary.

2 Prune by cutting the sideshoots off each stem so they each only have around five leaves, and taking out the tip of each stem once it has reached the end of its wire. For sources of more information on pruning and training, see Further Resources, page 140.

3 Kiwis can be further propagated by taking cuttings (see pages 136–7).

POMEGRANATE
Punica granatum

EASINESS: 🌢 **PATIENCE:** 🌢 **TYPE:** BUSH/TREE; PERENNIAL

Pomegranates make great houseplants, especially as they do not need the high humidity of some of the exotic fruits. They can grow into very large bushes or trees, but their size is easily controlled, and they are good subjects for bonsai. Ideally, sow the pips in April but any time of year is possible.

EQUIPMENT

- Pomegranate
- Kitchen towel
- Sieve
- Small (9cm) pot of compost
- Plastic bag and tie

STATS
SOW: INDOORS
GROW: INDOORS/OUTDOORS
MINIMUM
TEMPERATURE: 0°C
FULL HEIGHT: 2M

METHOD

① Pomegranate pips will be ripest if they are left in the fruit for about 2 weeks beyond the point at which they would normally be eaten, by which time the outer skin should be hard and wrinkly.

② Cut open the fruit and scoop out some of the 'jewels' – the juice sacs containing the pips. Selecting only whole ones, squeeze them individually on some kitchen towel to extract the pips. Wash them to remove all traces of fruit flesh – this is most easily done one by one under running water. Put a sieve underneath to prevent them being washed down the plughole if dropped. Sow the pips straight away, or dry and store them to sow later.

③ Sow the pips in a pot of pre-watered compost, and seal the pot in a plastic bag. Put it in a warm spot (21°C), ideally with a bit of heat at the base from a radiator or heated propagator (don't put it in the bag if using a propagator). Germination should take only 5–10 days.

④ Once the pips have sprouted, remove the bag and move the pot to a warm, sunny windowsill. Keep the compost moist.

CARE OF THE PLANT

1. The seedlings will be ready to repot when they are about 10cm tall, then repot as necessary. Pinch out the tips to promote a bushy shape, and keep pruned to restrict the size. Keep in a bright spot at room temperature, although they will tolerate cooler conditions.

2. Pomegranates are suitable for taking cuttings (see pages 136–7).

DATES
Phoenix dactylifera

EASINESS: 🌢 **PATIENCE:** 🌢🌢 **TYPE:** BUSH/TREE; PERENNIAL

Date pips grow into little palm trees. They develop slowly, so can be kept as unusual houseplants for many years. It's crucial to use fresh, unpitted dates – not dried – and preferably those that have not been sulphured or pasturised. Ideally, sow the pips in March but any time of year is possible.

EQUIPMENT
- Dates
- Jam jar or glass
- Plastic bag and tie
- Compost
- Small (9cm) pot (later)

STATS
SOW: INDOORS
GROW: INDOORS
MINIMUM
TEMPERATURE: 16°C
FULL HEIGHT: 1.5M

METHOD
1 Extract the pip from the fruit by scoring the date from top to bottom and peeling back the flesh, and wash it well.

2 Date pips have a hard outer coating: soften it by soaking for 48 hours in a jam jar or glass of water. Alternatively, dry the pips after washing, then rub the whole surface of the pip with sandpaper until rough.

3 Put a layer of moist compost in the bottom of a plastic food bag and lay the pips on top, then cover with more moist compost. Seal the bag then put it in a warm, dark place.

4 Check the bag daily for signs of growth, and wet the compost to keep it moist, but not soggy, as necessary. Roots may appear first, then shoots after 3–6 weeks.

CARE OF THE PLANT
1 Once a pip has produced a shoot, remove it from the bag and plant it in a small pot of compost, with the pip itself about 2–3cm below the surface.

2 Keep the plant on a warm, sunny windowsill out of draughts and take care not to over-water, especially in winter. Repot as required, putting it into only a slightly bigger pot each time. The plants will not need pruning.

DRAGON FRUIT (PITAYA)
Hylocereus undatus

EASINESS: 💧💧 **PATIENCE:** 💧💧 **TYPE:** TRAILING BUSH; PERENNIAL

The dragon fruit is one of the more exotic fruits and one of the more unusual pip plants: its scaly, pink globes are actually the product of a cactus plant. The flowers, if the pip plant can be induced to bear them, are massive (up to 30cm across in the wild), showy, fragrant affairs, but they only open at night. Ideally, sow the pips in April but any time of year is possible.

EQUIPMENT

- Dragon fruit
- Sieve and (muslin) cloth
- Plate
- Small (9cm) pot
- Compost and sand mix or cactus compost (see below)
- Plastic bag and tie

METHOD

1 Removing the flesh from the tiny pips is a fiddly affair; when wet, the pips will stick to everything. Scoop out some of the flesh and press it into a sieve lined with muslin. Wash under running water to separate the pips from the flesh and scrape out the pips to dry onto a plate.

2 Meanwhile, prepare the pot and compost. Specialist cacti compost mixes are available from garden centres and home stores, or make up a small quantity by mixing compost with sand and/or small-sized grit in a 50:50 ratio. Fill the pot, leaving a 1cm lip, and water.

3 Press the pips into the top of the compost, but do not cover them. Put the whole pot into a plastic bag and seal the top (or use a heated propagator), and keep in a bright, sunny spot at 18–21°C. Mist the surface of the compost with a spray bottle if it dries out.

4 The pips should germinate in 2–4 weeks; remove the bag at this point.

CARE OF THE PLANT

❶ Pot each plant into its own pot and repot as necessary – once they are established they will cope in a normal compost providing they don't sit in the wet. The cactus has long, thin stems that will either trail over the edge of the pot, or can be contained by training up a stake. Either cut off the stems when they reach the top, or allow them to flop over.

❷ Keep in a warm, bright spot.

STATS

SOW: INDOORS
GROW: INDOORS
MINIMUM
TEMPERATURE: 18°C
FULL HEIGHT: 1M

GRAPES
Vitis vinifera

EASINESS: 🌢🌢 **PATIENCE:** 🌢🌢🌢 **TYPE:** CLIMBER; PERENNIAL

Grapes are quite tricky to grow, but because the fruit contains so many pips, it's worth a try. In the wild, the pips would not germinate until after a long, cold winter, so mimicking this is necessary to ensure a better germination rate. Ideally, sow the pips in October or November and leave outside all winter, but any time of year is possible by using the fridge to break the dormancy.

EQUIPMENT

- Grapes
- Sieve
- Jam jar or glass
- Small (9cm) pot or tray of compost
- Plastic bag and tie or tray cover

METHOD

1 Wash the pips in a sieve, then soak the seeds for 24 hours in a jar or glass of water.

2 Sow in a pot or tray of pre-watered compost, and seal in a plastic bag, or put the cover over the tray to keep the compost moist. Store outside (protect from pests) or in the fridge for at least 6 weeks – the pips need to be kept at 1–3°C for all of this time. Check regularly that the compost is moist and water if required.

3 Once the (mock) winter is over, move the pot or tray into the warm. Room temperature (18–20°C), such as a sunny windowsill, is sufficient. The pips should germinate in 2–3 weeks; some may come up quickly, others may take much longer or not germinate at all.

CARE OF THE PLANT

1 Pot each seedling into its own small pot and keep in a sunny place (it doesn't matter if the room is cooler over winter). They will not require a lot of water, especially when dormant (after losing their leaves for winter), and can remain in that pot for up to a year before repotting.

2 Train the stems on to wires or a trellis, and prune in the winter back to a framework.

STATS
SOW: INDOORS/OUTDOORS
GROW: INDOORS/OUTDOORS
MINIMUM
TEMPERATURE: −10°C
FULL HEIGHT: 1.5M+

OLIVES
Olea europaea

EASINESS: ◗◗◗ **PATIENCE:** ◗◗◗ **TYPE:** BUSH/TREE; PERENNIAL

With a little patience, a home-grown olive grove is possible. Use fresh olives that haven't been treated or preserved at all. Otherwise, use olives that have only been preserved in oil, never brine (the salt will kill the viability of the pip). Ideally, sow the pips in October or November and leave outside all winter, but any time of year is possible by using the fridge to break the dormancy.

EQUIPMENT

- Olives
- Jam jar
- Sandpaper
- Small (9cm) pot of compost
- Netting and an elastic band for pots stored outside

STATS
SOW: INDOORS
GROW: INDOORS/OUTDOORS
MINIMUM
TEMPERATURE: −10°C
FULL HEIGHT: 1.5M+

METHOD

1 Olives can be tricky to grow from pips because they have two dormancy mechanisms, and it's necessary to break both of these before they are likely to germinate. The hard seed coat prevents water getting into the pip, and chemicals within the pip's coating inhibit germination.

2 Clean the pips of any flesh, then soak in a jam jar of water for 20 days. Discard any pips that float to the top – these will not be viable. Change the water every 3 days. This will start to soften the pip to allow water in.

3 Drain the pips. Once dry, carefully rub the pips all over with sandpaper. Don't take off too much – the idea is to remove the chemicals in the outer coating, not rub all the way through to the middle.

4 Sow in a pot of pre-watered compost. It now needs chilling for 2–3 months, either in the fridge or outside in winter. If the pot is to be stored outside, cover the top with netting and fix in place with an elastic band. Check regularly to ensure the compost is moist but not wet.

5 Move the pot to a windowsill or other spot at room temperature. Germination may still take up to 2 months.

CARE OF THE PLANT

1 Repot as necessary, finishing with as large a pot as there is space for. Once in its final pot, take out the tips of the branches every year to restrict their size. Olives are fairly hardy, providing their roots are not too wet and protected from frost in the cold months, so will grow happily outside or inside.

2 It is possible to take cuttings from an olive plant (see pages 136–7).

FIG
Ficus carica

EASINESS: 🌢🌢🌢 **PATIENCE:** 🌢🌢🌢 **TYPE:** TREE; PERENNIAL

Figs are are relatively straightforward to grow, if good pips can be obtained. The varieties 'Smyrna' or 'Calimyrna' are most likely to have fertile pips within them. Other varieties may not have been successfully pollinated. The fig tree is ideal for growing in a pot, as its roots are best restricted to limit its spread. Ideally, sow the pips in April but any time of year is possible.

EQUIPMENT
- Fig(s)
- Small bowl
- Slotted spoon or fork
- Small (9cm) pot of compost
- Plastic bag and tie

STATS
SOW: INDOORS
GROW: INDOORS/OUTDOORS
MINIMUM
TEMPERATURE: −10°C
FULL HEIGHT: 1.5M+

METHOD

❶ Separate the pips from the flesh by scooping the flesh into a bowl and adding water. Mash or squash the flesh by hand, and then leave it for an hour or so until the flesh has floated to the water's surface, and the pips have sunk to the bottom.

❷ Scrape off what's on the surface with a slotted spoon or fork and discard, then carefully pour off the water, leaving the rest of the fig pips and flesh in the bowl. Add more water and leave it overnight.

❸ In the morning, the remaining flesh should have floated away or dissolved from the pips at the bottom of the bowl. Discard any pips that have floated as they will not be viable.

❹ Sow the pips in a pot of pre-watered compost, put the whole pot in a plastic bag and tie at the top. Put the bag in a warm place (18–21°C) such as a sunny windowsill and check it daily to ensure the compost remains moist and to look for signs of growth. Germination should occur within 2 months but may be much faster.

❺ When the pips have developed shoots, remove the bag.

CARE OF THE PLANT

❶ Although a mature fig tree is hardy, the young plants will benefit from being protected from frosts if growing outdoors. Repot the seedlings as they grow, ending in a pot of 30–40cm diameter, and grow in a bright or sunny spot.

❷ Figs are vigorous growers, and will need pruning every year. Choose to grow the plant into a multi-stemmed bush shape, or select a single stem to grow straight up and then develop branches on the top as a standard.

PEANUT
Arachis hypogaea

EASINESS: ⬧ **PATIENCE:** ⬧ **TYPE:** BUSH; ANNUAL

Peanuts are not strictly a pip – nor indeed are they are a nut. In fact, they are a bean, but they are fun to grow, and worth including here. Get peanuts that have not been roasted and are still in their shells – often sold as 'monkey nuts' – and use a clear container to grow them in so the new nuts developing beneath the soil can be seen more easily. (This is why they are also known as 'ground nuts'.) Ideally, sow the pips in March but any time of year is possible.

EQUIPMENT

- Peanuts
- Jam jar or glass
- Knife or other flat implement
- Medium pot (clear plastic if possible)
- Compost

METHOD

❶ Choose peanuts that still have their shell intact – broken shells mean the nuts inside will have dried out – and discard any that seem overly dry or where the nut itself has already cracked in half. It's possible to plant the peanuts still in their shells, but germination will be faster if the shells are removed.

❷ To plant still in the shell, crack the shell open by pressing down on the shell with the flat blade of a knife or other flat implement. Then plant it as below.

❸ Otherwise, crack and remove the shells. Soak the peanuts (there should be two in each shell) in a jam jar or glass of water for 12 hours, discard any that float.

❹ Sow the peanuts in a pot of pre-watered compost – only a couple to a pot as they will need lots of surface space to grow. Put it in a warm, sunny place (21°C) and check daily if the compost needs watering. Germination should take 2–3 weeks.

CARE OF THE PLANT

1 Once the peanuts have germinated, select the strongest looking seedling per pot (short and sturdy is better than long and leggy) and pull out the other. Keep the pot in a warm, sunny spot and check the compost is always moist. It will not need any fertiliser.

2 The plant's leaves will fold up at night – this is natural and nothing to worry about. The plants won't need pruning. The pollinated flowers swell and start to grow downwards into the compost. Try to guide it to near the edge of the pot, because where it grows into the compost it will develop into a new peanut beneath the surface and you'll be able to see them through the clear pot.

STATS
SOW: INDOORS
GROW: INDOORS
MINIMUM
TEMPERATURE: 16°C
FULL HEIGHT: 0.3–0.6M

TOMATO
Lycopersicon esculentum

EASINESS: 🌢🌢 **PATIENCE:** 🌢 **TYPE:** BUSH/CLIMBER; ANNUAL

Tomato plants grown from pips are very likely to give a good harvest. Although the fruit could be any shape or size, the tomato they came from will be a good guide. Tomato plants grow in two different forms: vine (a tall, thin plant that needs tying up a sting or cane) and bush (a shorter, bushier plant that doesn't need training). Any commercially grown tomatoes will most likely be vine tomatoes. If anyone gives you some of their harvest, ask about the plants. Ideally, sow the pips in March but any time of year is possible.

EQUIPMENT

- Tomato
- Sieve
- Small bowl (optional, see below)
- Small (9cm) pot of compost

METHOD

❶ The warm, moist innards of a tomato are the ideal conditions in which its pips would germinate, so the pips are contained within a gelatinous coating that contains a chemical which inhibits this from happening. To get the pips to germinate, this coating has to be removed. There are two potential methods.

❷ The easiest method is to leave the fruit to ripen well beyond the point at which it would be good to eat, but before it goes mouldy. Scoop out the pips and juice from the middle of the fruit into a sieve and wash very thoroughly to remove all traces of juice and the coating. Tip the pips on to a plate to dry.

❸ Alternatively, ferment the coating away. Put the juice and pips into a small bowl, add water (about 50 per cent of the volume of the juice), and leave for 3 days, stirring twice daily. The mix will become covered in mould and/or start to bubble. Add the same volume of water again, and stir. Viable seeds will sink to the bottom, and the rest can be poured off the top. Rinse by adding more water, stirring and pouring off twice more before straining through a sieve and leaving to dry on a plate.

STATS

SOW: INDOORS
GROW: INDOORS/OUTDOORS
MINIMUM
TEMPERATURE: 10°C
FULL HEIGHT: 1.5M

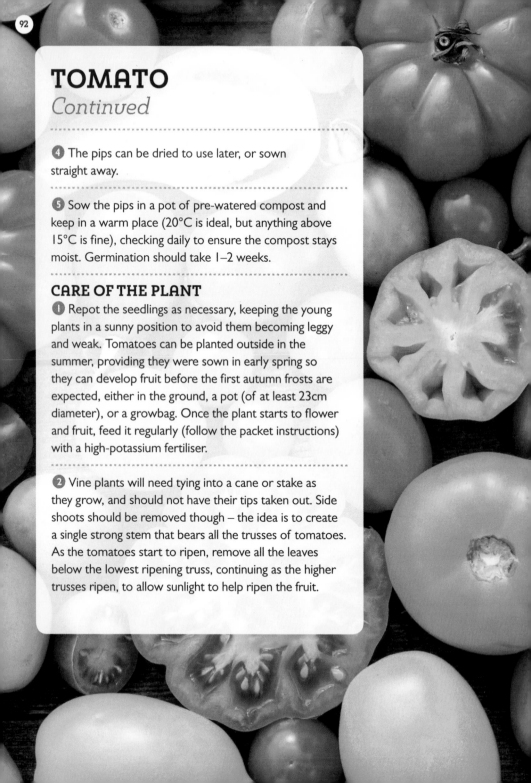

TOMATO
Continued

4 The pips can be dried to use later, or sown straight away.

5 Sow the pips in a pot of pre-watered compost and keep in a warm place (20°C is ideal, but anything above 15°C is fine), checking daily to ensure the compost stays moist. Germination should take 1–2 weeks.

CARE OF THE PLANT

1 Repot the seedlings as necessary, keeping the young plants in a sunny position to avoid them becoming leggy and weak. Tomatoes can be planted outside in the summer, providing they were sown in early spring so they can develop fruit before the first autumn frosts are expected, either in the ground, a pot (of at least 23cm diameter), or a growbag. Once the plant starts to flower and fruit, feed it regularly (follow the packet instructions) with a high-potassium fertiliser.

2 Vine plants will need tying into a cane or stake as they grow, and should not have their tips taken out. Side shoots should be removed though – the idea is to create a single strong stem that bears all the trusses of tomatoes. As the tomatoes start to ripen, remove all the leaves below the lowest ripening truss, continuing as the higher trusses ripen, to allow sunlight to help ripen the fruit.

PEPPER AND CHILLI PEPPER
Capsicum annuum

EASINESS: ◢ **PATIENCE:** ◢ **TYPE:** BUSH/PERENNIAL

The pips of peppers and chillies are easy to extract, and offer the possibility of a harvest of unusual fruits. The heat level will be an unknown factor with a pip-grown chilli, so it would be wise to be cautious when sampling any harvest. Ideally, sow the pips in March but any time of year is possible.

EQUIPMENT

- Pepper and/or chilli pepper
- Rubber gloves (for chilli peppers)
- Small (9cm) pot of compost
- Plastic bag and tie

METHOD

❶ Cut open the pepper, and (wearing rubber gloves for chilli peppers to protect from the spicy oil), rub the seeds off the white pith on to a plate. They can be sown straight away or dried and stored to sow later (use within a year).

❷ Sow the pips in a pot of pre-watered compost, and seal in a plastic bag. The pips will germinate at 18–21°C but benefit from some base heat, so put on a saucer on a radiator, or in a heated propagator. Keep the compost moist. They should germinate within 1–2 weeks; when shoots are seen, remove the bag. Keep in a warm, well-lit place.

CARE OF THE PLANT

❶ Plants grown outside will need protection from frosts. Ideally, sow in late winter/early spring inside. Repot the seedlings as necessary, and keep them in a sunny, warm position. Only move plants outside (either in a large pot or into the ground) once all risk of frost has passed.

❷ Keep the compost moist, and once the plants start to flower and fruit give them a regular feed of high-potassium fertiliser. Misting indoor-grown plants when they are flowering can help with pollination.

❸ The plant may need support, depending on how tall it grows. Don't take out the tip; the plant will branch naturally.

STATS

SOW: INDOORS
GROW: INDOORS/OUTDOORS
MINIMUM
TEMPERATURE: 10°C
FULL HEIGHT: 0.3—0.6M

PUMPKINS AND SQUASH
Cucurbita species

EASINESS: 🌢 **PATIENCE:** 🌢 **TYPE:** TRAILING BUSH/CLIMBER; ANNUAL

Anyone who's ever scraped out the middle of a pumpkin for a Halloween carving will know they contain plenty of pips. A plant sown from a pip will produce some form of pumpkin or squash, but the shape and taste of that fruit will depend on its genetic parents: it could be delicious or best reserved for carving. Ideally, sow the pips in April but any time of year is possible.

EQUIPMENT
- Pumpkin and/or squash
- Small (9cm) pot(s) or seed tray with modular insert of compost

STATS
SOW: INDOORS
GROW: INDOORS/OUTDOORS
MINIMUM
TEMPERATURE: 10°C
FULL HEIGHT: 2M+

METHOD
❶ Scrape the pips out of the fruit and wash well in a sieve, rubbing thoroughly to remove all traces of the flesh.

❷ Sow in individual pre-watered pots or cells of a modular seed tray, as the seedlings do not like their roots being disturbed. Keep at a minimum of 16°C, and ensure the compost does not dry out. Germination will take 1–2 weeks. The seedlings are relatively slow-growing, so start them early if they are to be planted outside as they will need all the time they can get before the first autumn frosts to produce and ripen any fruit.

CARE OF THE PLANT
❶ Move tray-sown seedlings into 9cm pots once they have filled the cell with roots. Once the plants have filled the pot, and all risk of frost has passed, plant in full sun in the ground or a large pot outdoors (or indoors). Ideally the plants will need temperatures of 18–21°C to grow well.

❷ The stems are long and trailing (with the exception of some summer squash plants, which are bushy), so could be trained up a wigwam or trellis to save space, if the fruits are supported with nets or old pairs of tights. They will not need pruning.

APPLES AND PEARS
Malus domestica and *Pyrus communis*

EASINESS: 🌢 **PATIENCE:** 🌢🌢🌢 **TYPE:** TREE; PERENNIAL

The fruit will not be the same as the original apple or pear, but there is something very satisfying about raising a tree from a tiny pip. Ideally, sow the pips in October or November and leave outside all winter, but any time of year is possible by using the fridge to break the dormancy.

EQUIPMENT
• Apple or pear
• Small (9cm) pot of compost
• Netting and an elastic band if sowing in a pot outside

STATS
SOW: INDOORS/OUTDOORS
GROW: INDOORS/OUTDOORS
MINIMUM
TEMPERATURE: −10°C
FULL HEIGHT: 2M+

METHOD
❶ Sow clean pips in a pot of pre-watered compost – put about five in a pot to increase your chances of success.

❷ The pips need a period of cold (less than 5°C for at least two months) to break their dormancy. Sow the pips in pots and leave them outdoors over winter, or put the pot in the fridge. If the pot is to be stored outside, stretch netting over the top, fixing in place with an elastic band, to prevent mice and other pests getting to the pips.

❸ After this time they can be moved to a warm, sunny windowsill (or left outside as spring develops), and should germinate within 3–8 weeks. Keep the compost consistently moist but not sodden.

CARE OF THE PLANT
❶ Plant the seedlings into their own pots, and keep repotting as they get bigger. If you can, plant them into the garden. They are fully hardy, and will require only some form of stake to support the young stem.

❷ When the tree is a year old, cut off the tip just above the fifth bud from the ground to encourage it to branch out. For more on pruning and training, see Further Resources, page 140.

PLUMS AND APRICOTS
Prunus domestica and *Prunus armeniaca*

EASINESS: 🌢 **PATIENCE:** 🌢🌢🌢 **TYPE:** TREE; PERENNIAL

Plums and apricots are a long-term investment, but more likely to produce decent fruit than apple pips. Ideally, sow the pips in October or November and leave outside all winter, but any time of year is possible by using the fridge to break the dormancy.

EQUIPMENT

- Plum or apricot
- Jam jar or glass
- Small (9cm) pot of compost
- Netting and an elastic band if sowing in a pot outside

STATS

SOW: INDOORS/OUTDOORS
GROW: INDOORS/OUTDOORS
MINIMUM
TEMPERATURE: −10°C
FULL HEIGHT: 2M+

METHOD

1 Clean the pip, removing all traces of the flesh, and, to soften the hard outer shell and allow water to penetrate, soak it for 48 hours in a jar or glass of water.

2 Sow in a pot of pre-watered compost, and leave it to chill either in the fridge or outside in wintertime for 2–3 months to induce them to germinate. If the pot is to be kept outside, cover the top with netting and fix in place with an elastic band to protect it from mice and other pests.

3 Move the pot to a warm, sunny spot (or leave outside for springtime), where it should germinate within a few months, but may take as long as 18 months.

CARE OF THE PLANT

1 Keep repotting the young tree as it gets bigger. If possible, plant plum trees out into the garden in a sheltered, sunny spot, tying into a stake to prevent wind damage. When the tree is a year old, cut off the tip just above the fifth bud from the ground to encourage it to branch out.

2 Apricots prefer being grown in the shelter of a greenhouse or conservatory, where they can be trained against a wall rather than grown as a standard tree (see Further Resources, page 140, for more information).

PEACHES AND NECTARINES
Prunus persica and *Prunus persica* var. *nectarina*

EASINESS: 🌢 **PATIENCE:** 🌢🌢🌢 **TYPE:** TREE; PERENNIAL

It will take a peach or nectarine pip about 4 or 5 years to grow into a tree big enough to bear fruit. Ideally, sow the pips in October or November and leave outside all winter, but any time of year is possible by using the fridge to break the dormancy.

EQUIPMENT

- Peach or nectarine
- Small (9cm) pot of compost
- Netting and an elastic band for pots going outside

STATS

SOW: INDOORS/OUTDOORS
GROW: INDOORS/OUTDOORS
MINIMUM
TEMPERATURE: −10°C
FULL HEIGHT: 2M+

METHOD

❶ Clean the pips to remove all traces of the flesh, and leave to dry on a sunny windowsill for 3 days.

❷ Sow the pips in pots of pre-watered compost, putting only one per pot as they dislike root disturbance. Chill the pots in the fridge for 2–3 months, or outside over winter, making sure the compost remains consistently moist. Protect pots outside from pests by covering with netting fixed in place with an elastic band.

❸ After the (mock) winter, move the pot to a sunny windowsill, where temperatures are 15–20°C. If possible, supply some base heat by putting the pot on a saucer on a radiator or in a heated propagator. Make sure the compost does not dry out. The pips should germinate within a couple of months.

CARE OF THE PLANT

❶ Keep the seedling in a pot for a year (but repot if the roots start growing out of the bottom of the pot), and tie in the young stem to a cane to ensure straight upright growth. After a year move it to its final pot or place in the garden, and stake it to prevent wind damage.

❷ Peaches are ideal for training against a south- or west-facing wall or fence (see Further Resources, page 140).

CHERRIES
Prunus cerasus

EASINESS: 🌢 **PATIENCE:** 🌢🌢🌢 **TYPE:** TREE; PERENNIAL

Cherry trees are worth growing for their spring blossom alone, but many also have colourful autumn foliage. The pips' size makes them easy to see being dispersed in bird droppings through mid- to late summer. Ideally, sow the pips in September or October and leave outside all winter, but any time of year is possible by using the fridge to break the dormancy.

EQUIPMENT
- Cherries
- Sieve
- Small (9cm) pot of compost
- Netting and an elastic band if sowing n a pot outside

STATS
SOW: INDOORS/OUTDOORS
GROW: INDOORS/OUTDOORS
MINIMUM
TEMPERATURE: −10°C
FULL HEIGHT: 2M+

METHOD

❶ Wash the pips to remove the flesh by pushing them around in a sieve under running water.

❷ Sow the pips in a pot of pre-watered compost – as the wait can be a long time, several pips to one pot will reduce the storage space; just space them equally around the circumference. If the pot is going to be stored outside over winter, cover the top with netting, fixed in place with an elastic band, to prevent mice stealing the pips.

❸ Keep the pot in a cold place – outside or in the fridge (0–5°C) – for 3 months, then move to a warm spot such as a sunny windowsill and wait for the pips to put out shoots. Germination should take place within a couple of months.

CARE OF THE PLANT

❶ Once the pips have small shoots, they can be extracted carefully and moved into individual small pots. Repot as necessary, ultimately planting out into a sunny place in the garden or a large pot.

❷ Support the young trees with a cane or stake. They are fully hardy and can stay outside all year round. For more on pruning and training, see Further Resources, page 140.

GOOSEBERRIES, REDCURRANTS, BLACKCURRANTS AND WHITECURRANTS
Ribes species

EASINESS: 🌢 **PATIENCE:** 🌢🌢 **TYPE:** BUSH; PERENNIAL

Currant and gooseberry bushes grow easily from pips, and will bear fruit at least good enough for jam if not for desserts. Ideally, sow the pips in October or November and leave outside all winter, but any time of year is possible by using the fridge to break the dormancy.

EQUIPMENT

- Gooseberry redcurrant/ blackcurrant/ whitecurrant
- Sieve and muslin cloth
- Small (9cm) pot of compost
- Netting and an elastic band if sowing in a pot outside

STATS
SOW: INDOORS/OUTDOORS
GROW: INDOORS/OUTDOORS
MINIMUM
TEMPERATURE: −10°C
FULL HEIGHT: 1M+

METHOD 1

1 Squeeze the flesh and pips out of the skins into a sieve lined with muslin and wash to remove the pips from the flesh. Drying them on a plate for a few hours will make them easier to handle, but they can be sown straight away.

2 Sow the pips into a pot of pre-watered compost, and cover with netting to protect from pests (fix in place with an elastic band) if it is to be stored outside. Put the pot in a cold place for 2–3 months, either outside over winter or in the fridge.

3 Move the pot to a warm, sunny spot after the (mock) winter. Germination should take place within a couple of months.

CARE OF THE PLANT

1 Once the seedlings are in individual pots, they will grow quite quickly. Repot as necessary, and plant out into the garden or a larger pot once they are a year old. All currant and gooseberry plants are fully hardy, and will tolerate a partially shady spot.

2 Currants and gooseberries can be left to grow in a more or less natural bush shape, with some pruning to restrict their size, or (with the exception of blackcurrants) trained as a standard or cordon. For more information on pruning and training fruit bushes, see Further Resources, page 140.

3 These plants are suitable for making cuttings (see pages 136–7).

BLUEBERRIES AND CRANBERRIES
Vaccinium species

EASINESS: **PATIENCE:** **TYPE:** BUSH; PERENNIAL

Blueberries and cranberries will only grow well in acidic soil, so ensure the soil has a low pH reading (testing kits are available from garden centres). Otherwise, a pot filled with ericaceous compost will serve just as well. Ideally, sow the pips in October or November and leave outside all winter, but any time of year is possible by using the fridge to break the dormancy.

EQUIPMENT

- Blueberries and/or cranberries
- Sieve and muslin cloth
- Small (9cm) pot of ericaceous compost
- Netting and an elastic band if sowing in a pot outside

STATS

SOW: INDOORS/OUTDOORS
GROW: INDOORS/OUTDOORS
MINIMUM TEMPERATURE: −10°C
FULL HEIGHT: 1M+

METHOD

1 Squash the fruit into a sieve lined with muslin and wash to extract the pips.

2 Sow the pips into a pot of pre-watered compost. Fix netting over the top with an elastic band if the pot is to be stored outside; this will protect the pips from mice and other pests. Store in the fridge or outside (temperatures of 0–5°C) for 2–3 months, ensuring the compost stays moist but not sodden.

3 Move the pot to a warm place such as a sunny windowsill. Germination should take place within 2 months.

CARE OF THE PLANT

1 Repot as necessary, always using ericaceous compost. Water using rainwater if possible – tap water will raise the pH of the compost. If the compost or soil is too alkaline, the plants will show it as their leaves turn yellow. Adding some sulphur (available from the garden centre) can help redress the balance.

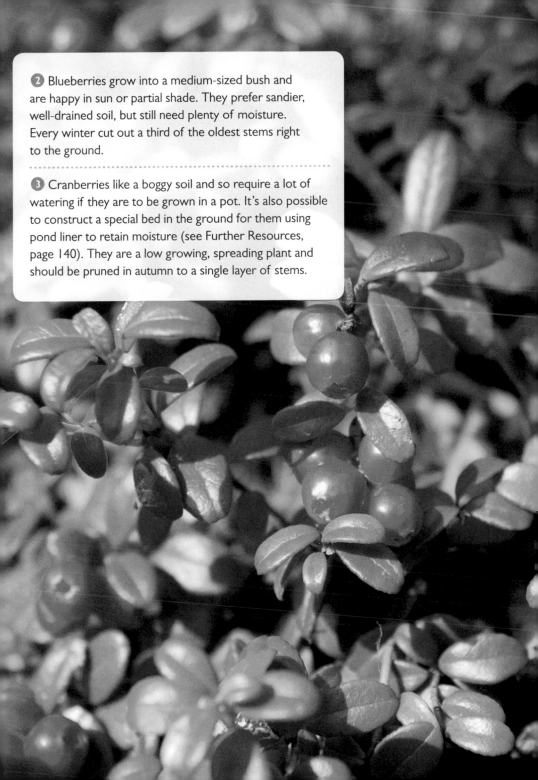

2 Blueberries grow into a medium-sized bush and are happy in sun or partial shade. They prefer sandier, well-drained soil, but still need plenty of moisture. Every winter cut out a third of the oldest stems right to the ground.

3 Cranberries like a boggy soil and so require a lot of watering if they are to be grown in a pot. It's also possible to construct a special bed in the ground for them using pond liner to retain moisture (see Further Resources, page 140). They are a low growing, spreading plant and should be pruned in autumn to a single layer of stems.

STRAWBERRIES, RASPBERRIES AND BLACKBERRIES

Fragaria species and *Rubus species*

EASINESS: ◗ **PATIENCE:** ◗◗ **TYPE:** BUSH; PERENNIAL

Berry plants germinate and grow faster than other fruits, and are also likely to produce fruit themselves. All can be grown in a pot, but raspberries and blackberries will be happier in the ground. Ideally, sow strawberry pips in March but any time of year is possible. Raspberry and blackberry pips can also be sown all year round by using a fridge to break the dormancy.

EQUIPMENT

- Strawberries/ raspberries/ blackberries
- Knife
- Sieve and muslin cloth
- Small (9cm) pot of compost
- Netting and an elastic band if sowing in a pot outside

STATS

SOW: INDOORS/OUTDOORS
GROW: INDOORS/OUTDOORS
MINIMUM TEMPERATURE: −10°C
FULL HEIGHT: 0.3–2M+

METHOD

❶ Strawberry pips are easy to locate – they are the only pip borne on the outside of the fruit, where they influence the ultimate size of the fruit through the chemicals they contain. Pick them off with the point of a knife and wash in a sieve lined with muslin if they still have any bits of fruit on them.

❷ Sow in a pot of pre-watered compost and put in a warm spot, checking daily if the compost needs re-moistening. The pips should germinate in 4 weeks.

❸ Raspberry and blackberry pips are within each individual juicy cell that makes up the overall fruit. Squash the fruit into a sieve lined with muslin and wash off the flesh to extract the pips.

❹ The pips will need a period of 1 month in the cold, so after sowing in a pot of pre-watered compost, put the pot in the fridge, ensuring that the compost remains moist at all times. Once out of the fridge, move the pot to a warm spot and the pips should germinate within a month.

STRAWBERRIES, RASPBERRIES AND BLACKBERRIES
Continued

CARE OF THE PLANT (STRAWBERRIES)

① Once germinated, the pips can be a bit slow to start growing, but once they have got going will quickly get bigger. Repot the seedlings as necessary – a single plant will need a final pot size of 1.5–2l, more can be planted in a larger pot, or plant them in the ground. Keep in a sunny spot, but not too warm – 20°C is optimal – but make sure they get a cold spell over winter otherwise they will not flower. They will happily grow outside.

② Strawberries are especially prone to Botrytis (grey mould, see page 129), so it's important to remove any old leaves and stems to keep the plant tidy, but no further pruning is required.

③ Hopefully the plant will produce fruit, after which it will put out runners – long stems with tiny plantlets along their length. To create more plants, pin down the plantlet nearest the original plant into a 9cm pot of pre-watered compost using bent-out paperclips. Cut off the stem beyond this plantlet and keep the compost moist. The plantlet will soon take root in the pot, after which it can be severed from the original plant. This can be repeated for the first plantlet on each of the stems and is a very quick way to multiply a stock of strawberry plants.

(RASPBERRIES AND BLACKBERRIES)

❶ These produce flowers and fruit on tall stems that need tying in to wires or, if growing in a pot, a wigwam. Repot the seedlings as they grow, finishing in as large a pot as possible (no more than three plants to a 30cm diameter pot), or ideally planting out into the ground. Grow in a sunny spot, although they will tolerate partial shade.

❷ Every autumn, cut out the stems that have already produced fruit back to the ground and tie in the new shoots.

CHAPTER 4
LOOKING AFTER PLANTS AS THEY GROW

Getting the pips to germinate is only half the fun – watching them grow into proper plants is the best bit. Having a house full of plants more usually found on Mediterranean hillsides or in tropical jungles, or a garden bursting with fruit and vegetables produced from kitchen scraps, is immensely satisfying.

This chapter covers the tasks of looking after the growing plants: moving them into bigger pots or the ground outside, and how to prune, support and multiply them as they grow.

The most common pests, diseases and other problems they may fall foul of are explained too: find out what to look out for and how to deal with it, and how to avoid the plants getting infected in the first place.

REPOTTING

Once the pips have germinated, they will need moving into a pot of their own, and from there, another one, two or more pots as they grow. It's important not to move a plant into a much bigger pot at any stage; a large quantity of compost will hold a lot of water, which can swamp a small rootball.

MOVING SEEDLINGS FROM TRAYS

Increase the pot size gradually, and you will also be giving the plant regular fresh compost. Once mature, a plant can be kept in the same pot year-on-year. Just repot it every 1–3 years as below, brushing off as much old compost as possible and replacing with new. Whatever size plant you are putting into a new pot, ensure the plant has been well watered a few hours before moving it.

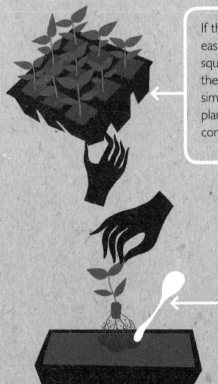

If the pip was sown in a module cell it is much easier to move. Using a thumb and forefinger, squeeze the underneath of the cell tray to push the plug of compost and roots upwards, while simultaneously pulling very gently on a leaf of the plant. Once it's out of the tray handle the root/compost plug (again, gently) rather than the plant.

If the pip was one of many sown in a single tray, hold on to a leaf and gently pull the plant at the same time as using a pencil or teaspoon handle (both adequate makeshift dibbers) to lever up the roots from the compost.

TAKING A PLANT OUT OF A POT

Cover the top of the pot by spreading a hand over it, with some fingers either side of the plant's stem. Use the other hand to hold the pot and turn it upside down, pulling the pot off the rootball. Don't worry if some loose compost falls away, just hold the rootball intact.

If the plant is large enough to be moved from a pot that is too big to lift as above, it will by now be strong enough to withstand being held by the stem and pulled gently upwards, having used a trowel or spade to lever out and support the rootball first.

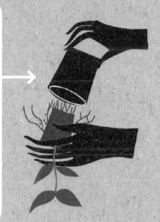

PUTTING THE PLANT IN A NEW POT

Hold the plant in the new pot to estimate the depth of compost needed underneath it — the top of the rootball should be 1–2cm from the top of the pot to leave a lip for watering.

Remove the plant and fill in the bottom of the pot to slightly above that depth, then tap the pot down a few times to settle the compost.

Put the plant on top, still holding on to it to keep it centred, and fill in around the sides of the rootball with more compost. Overfill it slightly. Tap the pot, then carefully firm it all together, pushing only on the new compost, not around the base of the rootball. A gentle tug on a leaf, or the stem of bigger plants, should not dislodge the plant from the pot. Water the pot well.

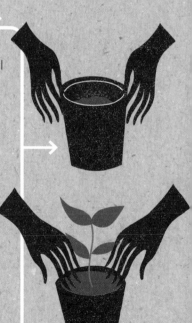

PLANTING OUT

Transferring a plant from a pot to the ground outside is called 'planting out'. Before doing this it is important to ensure the plant is ready to be moved. Taking it from a warm windowsill indoors to a cold patch of ground could set back its growth or even kill it. It's best to plant out in spring: the weather is warm but the ground is not too dry as it can be in summer.

First the plant should be 'hardened off'. This process simply means to acclimatise the plant to outdoor life gradually. Put the pot outside only in the daytime at first, bringing it back inside at night. After a few days it can be left outside overnight, but with a bit of protection such as horticultural fleece or newspaper over the top of it for extra insulation. Once it has been outside like this for a few more days it will be ready to plant in the ground. Make sure it has had a good watering a few hours before planting.

Prepare the ground first (see page 38). If it is dry, water the ground around the planting spot, too.

The planting hole should be as deep as the rootball, so that the top of the rootball is level with the ground, and twice as wide.

Take the plant out of its pot (see page 117) and place it in the hole. Backfill the soil around the rootball and firm down, taking care not to press around the base of the stem itself, which might break off the roots. Tugging gently on the plant should not pull it out of the ground.

Water the plant and the ground around it well, and continue to keep checking if it needs watering every day for a few weeks. Until the plant is able to grow its roots out into the new ground to seek water, it is essentially still in a pot and will need this extra care until it can get established.

It may also be necessary to put netting or a cloche over the top of the plant to protect it from pests, or to put in a stake for climbing plants or trees.

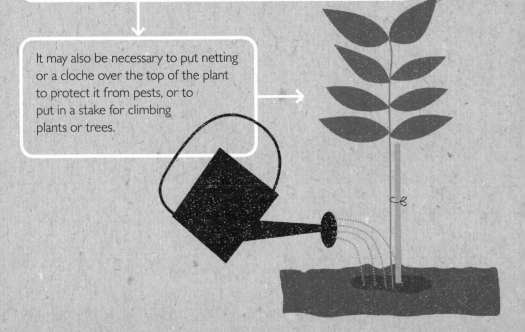

KEEPING PLANTS TO SIZE

All the pips will start off as a single stem, and most would continue that way given the option, it being the fastest way to grow up towards the light. To give the plant a more attractive appearance – such as a rounded dome full of leaves, or a well-branched tree – some pruning will be necessary.

PRUNING

When pruning is carried out will depend on how fast the plant grows. Generally it is only plants that will form trees, shrubs and climbers that will need pruning, although some annuals benefit from having the tips removed to create bushier plants.

REMOVING THE TIP

Removing the growing tip of a stem (the tip of the stem and topmost leaf or pair of leaves) will encourage the plant to produce side shoots and branches. As these branches get larger, their tips can also be taken off to encourage even more side shoots.

Use sharp, clean tools such as secateurs, scissors or a knife. Always cut the stem just above the topmost leaf that will remain on the stem so there is not a stub of leafless stem left on the plant (this is both ugly and susceptible to infection).

CUT HERE TO TAKE OUT THE TIP

CUT HERE TO TAKE OUT THE TIP OF THE MAIN STEM

CUT HERE TO TAKE OUT THE TIPS OF THE SIDE BRANCHES

Once the plant is fully mature, it can be trimmed regularly (once or twice a year after flowering) to stop it outgrowing its space. At this time any dead branches can be taken off as well, following the same principle of cutting it just above a healthy leaf or back to a healthy stem.

Pruning climbers follows the same principle as pruning bushy plants: taking off the top of the main stem will encourage the plant to produce more side shoots. In climbers, the side shoots provide more opportunity for it to flower and perhaps produce fruit, but it is best done once the plant has already attained some height.

Fruit trees such as apples, plums and cherries can be pruned and trained in many ways. For more information, see Further Resources, page 140.

APICAL DOMINANCE

This is the mechanism in the plant that dictates the main stem will grow fastest and tallest to the detriment of side branches. If the tip is removed, the growth hormones are redirected to form side shoots.

SUPPORTING TALL PLANTS AND CLIMBERS

Depending on the type of plant (see the individual pip for specific growing information), it could be supported by a single stake or cane, ramble over a wigwam or be trained along a wire or wires.

TYING IN

It is important to provide adequate support to a climbing plant, especially in the early stages of growth. Trying to untangle a mop of long stems and tie them up is more difficult and usually results in damaging some of the shoots.

When putting in a cane or stake, ideally put it in before the plant, otherwise put it near but not right next to the stem where it could damage the roots as it is being inserted. Push it all the way to the base of the pot, or about 60cm into the ground, to ensure it can take the weight of the stem.

Tie in the stem to the support using a figure-of-eight loop, with the stem in one circle of the eight and the support in the other, tying it off against the support rather than the stem. Make the loops just below a leaf or pair of leaves: this will give the tie something to support and hide it from view. It should be only just tight enough to hold the stem to the support, allowing some room for the stem to grow wider.

Ties should be checked every month or so to make sure they are not getting too tight. Replace tight or broken ties as necessary, or remove them if they are no longer needed to support the plant.

Use a soft garden twine if possible. Twine is soft on the stem of the plant so will not rub and damage it, and (unlike wire or rubber ties) will also degrade over time so is less likely to strangle the stem as it grows wider.

PESTS

Unfortunately there are legions of minibeasts – and not-so-mini-beasts – who will be attracted to the pip plants, even on an urban windowsill. Protecting them is easy, but not always attractive. The worst culprits, and methods of dealing with them, are below, but see also Further Resources (page 140), for more information on identifying pests.

PREVENTION IS BETTER THAN CURE.

Keeping plants healthy – well watered, fertilised and in the right position – will help them fight off attacks from bugs and other pests. Catching an infestation early increases the chances of getting rid of it entirely, so check plants regularly. It's also crucial to check any other plants that are in the house, or being brought into the house, for pests that could spread to the pip plants. Use chemical pesticides only as a last resort, after trying the other control methods, and always select a treatment that is recommended for the problem. Read the label and make sure that all manufacturer's instructions are followed, including maximum dose, spray and harvest intervals.

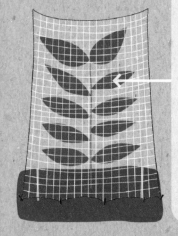

Big pests: Outside, this could be birds, mice, squirrels, rabbits or even deer, plus the usual household pets that can also do damage inside.

Signs of damage: Large holes or tearing of leaves, stems, or whole plants where they have been eaten or just chewed. Cats will scratch up bare soil, uncovering pips, and mice and squirrels will also eat pips in pots or the ground. Rabbits like to gnaw the bark from young stems.

Control: Physical barriers such as fencing, netting, horticultural fleece or cloches (plastic or glass) will keep most things off plants in the ground; thorny sticks can be spread over ground to deter cats; and netting can be tightly secured over pots to keep out mice and squirrels.

Aphids: A large group of small flies that take the sap from plants' leaves and stems, including the most common, greenfly and blackfly. Whitefly is not an aphid, but the damage and control is much the same.

Signs of damage: Wilting, curling or distorted leaves, a sticky sheen on the upperside of leaves, often later covered with a black mould. Clusters of the bugs on the undersides of leaves and around leaf shoots, especially on the newest growth. Whitefly will come off the plant in a cloud if disturbed.

Control: Physical removal by washing or picking them off (don't just wash off on to the soil, they'll climb back up; make sure they go down the plughole). There are various proprietary sprays available that will kill off most bugs, and insecticidal soaps can be used to wash plants as well. Outside, encourage blue tits, ladybirds, hoverflies and other predators to the garden as natural pest controllers.

Slugs and snails: Easily identified, although there are many, many different species of varying sizes that can hide in the smallest of spaces before coming out at dusk to feed.

Signs of damage: Holes in leaves, or leaves and stems of younger plants eaten entirely. A shiny, sticky trail where they have moved about is often visible on the plant and soil.

Control: Physical removal is best done at dusk or in the early morning for the highest success rate. The undersides of pots and trays are favoured hiding places. Organic pellets are reasonably effective, but other barriers (coffee grounds, eggshells, copper bands, etc.) less so. Outside, frogs, toads and many birds all eat slugs and snails, so encourage them into the garden.

Caterpillars: Another obvious pest, that is more visible during the day. Myriad size, colour and hairiness variations.

Signs of damage: Holes in leaves, or leaves eaten away entirely. Caterpillars and their excrement visible on the leaves and stems.

Control: Prevent the butterflies from laying their eggs on the plant with netting. Otherwise, pick off the caterpillars and wash the excrement off the leaves. Some chemical sprays will work on caterpillars.

Mealybug: An indoor pest which, once it takes hold, is very hard to eradicate. The small bugs live on the undersides of leaves and in the joins between leaf and stem, from where they suck the sap of the plant. Their grey, fluffy, waxy exterior makes them impervious to being washed or sprayed off, and their habit of living in the most inaccessible parts of the plant makes them difficult to remove.

Signs of damage: The plant can become stunted and generally unhealthy. The tops of leaves become coated in the clear, sticky excrement of the bugs.

Control: Pick off all those bugs that can be seen, and blast plants that will withstand it with the shower to try and dislodge others (again, make sure they are washed away completely). Chemical treatments are also available. It may be necessary to tolerate a low-level infestation to keep the plant, with regular removal of the bugs as they multiply.

DISEASES

Plant diseases split broadly into three groups: fungal, bacterial and viruses. Fungal diseases are much more common than bacterial diseases, especially on indoor plants. These are the diseases most likely to affect pip plants. If the symptoms don't match these descriptions, check Further Resources (page 140) for more information about what may be ailing the plant.

A HEALTHY ENVIRONMENT

As with preventing pests, infection is much less likely on healthy plants, so look after the pips well. Good housekeeping is also important to avoid cultivating an atmosphere in which disease could take hold, and to avoid spreading any existing disease. Keep plants tidy, removing dead leaves and other detritus around the base of the plant. Make sure tools and equipment – including the pots themselves – are clean by washing with soap or other detergent and hot water. If the plant's compost develops mould on its surface, repot it, washing off the roots entirely before replanting in fresh compost.

Fungicidal sprays are available to treat some diseases, but are best reserved for only when they are absolutely necessary. Select a treatment that is recommended for the disease you have identified and always read the label before choosing a product. Make sure all manufacturer's instructions are followed, including maximum dose, spray and harvest intervals.

Botrytis: A fungal disease also known as grey mould. It is so prevalent that spores are always present in the air, everywhere, so keeping plants healthy and not vulnerable to infection is crucial. Tends to infect dead or weak parts of the plant first, then spread to healthy tissue.

Signs of damage: A fluffy grey mould develops quickly on infected parts, often at the base of the plant first, and spreads rapidly through the plant. Can appear as spots on flower petals.

Control: Prevent infection by ensuring good air circulation around the plant, and that all dead or damaged plant material is removed promptly. Snags and tears should be tidied to a neat cut with sharp tools to minimise the area of open wounds. If grey mould does take hold, remove and dispose of all infected parts as soon as possible, trying to contain it in the process to avoid clouds of spores being released.

Mildew: There are two types of mildew: powdery and downy, which describe the type of white mould that develops on leaf surfaces. Both are fungal diseases.

Signs of damage: Patches of white mould develop on leaf surfaces, spreading ultimately to the whole plant. Powdery mildew is visible on the upperside of the leaf; downy on the underside, with corresponding yellow patches above. Leaves can turn yellow and die, and growth is hampered.

Control: Powdery mildew is often caught by plants that have dry roots but humidity around their leaves. Correct watering and good air circulation will help prevent infection. Downy mildew tends to infect younger plants, but is also characteristic of damp environments. Remove infected parts of the plant as soon as they are seen and improve the atmosphere around them to limit the spread.

Viruses: These tend to be brought in via the plant itself — sometimes even in the pips — or through infected pests or tools.

Signs of damage: Yellow spots or streaks on the leaves, and a general stunting or distorted growth of the whole plant.

Control: Once established, viruses are impossible to treat, so the plant is best disposed of to avoid infecting others. Clean tools and equipment thoroughly afterwards to avoid spreading the disease.

PROBLEMS

As well as pests and diseases, there are a few problems the pip plants may suffer from. All are easily rectified by changing the way the plant is cared for.

UNDER-WATERING

Symptoms: The leaves, and ultimately stems, will start to become floppy, thin and drooping. Older leaves will yellow and fall off, flower buds will fall or fail to open. The compost or soil will be dry as dust.

Remedy: Water! Stand the pot in a larger tub or bucket of water – it may need watering from the top as well or weighing down if it floats – until the compost is soaked through. Remove and allow the excess water to drain away. Check it more regularly in future.

OVER-WATERING

Symptoms: Similar to under-watering, but the compost will be sodden. The leaves may develop raised bumps, which can later turn brown and corky (a 'disease' called oedema), if the plant is taking up more water than it can cope with.

Remedy: Stop watering until the compost is only moist, not sodden. Don't remove any leaves; they will be needed to help lose the excess water through evaporation. Improve the drainage of the pot or soil if possible – pots should not be left standing in water.

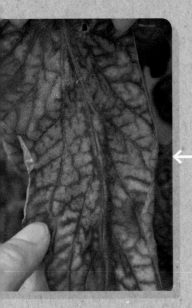

NUTRIENT DEFICIENCY

Symptoms: The effect depends on which nutrients are deficient. The most common is nitrogen, which will show as a general yellowing of the leaves, starting with the oldest leaves first. Potassium deficiency will show as poor flowering and fruiting, phosphorus-deficient plants will have a blueish tinge and poor root development. Magnesium deficiency is also quite common and also shows as a yellowing of the leaves, but the veins of the leaf remain green.

Remedy: Apply fertiliser rich in the appropriate nutrient, always within the dosage and frequency advised on the packet.

LEAF SCORCH

Symptoms: The edges of the leaves turn brown and crispy; they have died off suddenly. This is due to extremes of either heat or cold, the latter usually caused by a frost.

Remedy: The damaged leaves cannot be saved, so allow them to fall off naturally (the plant may still be withdrawing some nutrients out of them so don't pick them off), then dispose of them. Shelter the plant from the temperature extreme: move it back from a sunny windowsill or away from the radiator to protect it from heat. In the cold, move it under cover or indoors if possible. If it has to stay outside, find the warmest spot for it – heating vents on buildings create microclimates of warmer conditions in a cold garden for example – and/or cover it with horticultural fleece or newspaper (at night, it needs some sunlight in the day).

PHYSICAL DAMAGE:

Symptoms: Broken branches or stems, from animals, the wind or other knocks.

Remedy: Cut off the broken sections using sharp tools to make a clean cut below the damaged section. Wounds are vulnerable to infection before they can heal over, so the aim is to make it as small and neat as possible.

TAKING CUTTINGS

Taking cuttings from a plant to create new ones is an alternative to growing from a pip. Having grown, for example, a citrus tree from a pip, a small section of stem can be removed and planted into compost. It will develop its own roots and, in time, grow into a plant that is genetically identical to the one it was taken from (a clone).

Growing from cuttings is a faster method than sowing from pips, and allows the original pip plants to be multiplied when they themselves may not produce fruit. Domestic gardeners usually only take cuttings from perennial plants, i.e. not annuals such as tomatoes, once they are well-established and big enough. However, commerical growers will use cuttings to perpetuate the characteristics of named varieties.

This is a general introduction to taking cuttings – there are many forms of cuttings and means of taking them – for sources of more detailed information, see Further Resources (page 140).

TAKING A CUTTING

Choose a healthy section of stem that is still pliable, either from the main shoot or a side shoot. More than one cutting can be taken from a plant – if it needs pruning anyway, why not use what is removed to make cuttings?

The section of stem should be about 10cm long. Cut the bottom end on an angle and just below a leaf or pair of leaves (remove the stub that's left on the plant). Cut off the leaves on the lower half of the stem section.

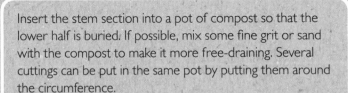

Insert the stem section into a pot of compost so that the lower half is buried. If possible, mix some fine grit or sand with the compost to make it more free-draining. Several cuttings can be put in the same pot by putting them around the circumference.

As the cuttings have no roots, it's important they do not dry out. The compost should be kept moist but not sodden (which may lead to the cuttings rotting), and be kept in a propagator or have a plastic bag over the top of the pot to keep the air around them humid.

Remove the bag or lid daily to circulate the air and check the cuttings. Those that have successfully rooted will eventually put out new shoots from the stem, those that fail will either rot or dry out and should be thrown away as soon as it's evident they have not survived.

Rooted cuttings can be taken out of the pot if they are sharing it with others or left to grow on until they need repotting (see pages 116–17).

GLOSSARY

Annual A plant that completes its life cycle within a year, growing from seed to flowering then dying off. For example, tomatoes and pumpkins.

Apical dominance The mechanism in the plant that dictates the main stem will grow fastest and tallest instead of the side branches. If the tip is removed, the growth hormones are redirected to form side shoots.

Bonsai The art of growing miniature trees in containers.

Cloche A structure to go over a plant to protect it from cold temperatures and/or pests. Can be bell-shaped, a box or tunnel and made from plastic or glass.

Cordon A means of training a plant, usually fruit trees or bushes, into a single stem with short side-shoots that bear the fruit. Useful for fitting in a lot of plants to a small space.

Cotyledon Stores of energy within the seed used in germination. Also known as 'seed leaf'.

Cutting A small piece of stem and leaves removed from the plant and potted in the hope that it will produce roots and grow into a new plant. Plants multiplied in this way will be genetically identical.

Dicotyledon A flowering plant that has two seed leaves.

Dibber A cylindrical tool, usually with a point at one end, used for making holes in the soil/compost for inserting seeds, or for levering the roots of seedlings being repotted out of the compost.

Dormancy A means of seed survival over a (long) period of time. A seed that is dormant will not germinate until it experiences the correct environmental conditions.

Endosperm A store of food within the seed for the new plant to use for energy during germination.

Embryo The new plant in miniature, encased within the seed, including the radicle and plumule.

Ericaceous compost A growing medium that is acidic in its make up and therefore suitable for plants that like acidic conditions. Often sold as 'Rhododendron and Camellia compost'.

Establish(ed) A plant that is established has put out roots into the compost or soil it is growing in, and is able to take up water and nutrients. Repotted or recently planted-out plants will take time to establish in their new situation.

Germination When a seed takes in water and grows a root and shoot.

Hardening off The process of acclimatising a plant to new surroundings, usually when taken from inside to outdoors.

Monocotyledon A plant with only one seed leaf, such as all grasses.

Perennial A plant that lives from year to year.

pH The measure of the acidity or alkalinity of the soil. A pH of 7 is neutral, less is acidic, more is alkaline. Most plants prefer a pH of 6–7.

Photosynthesis The plant's process of turning water and carbon dioxide into food using the energy from the sun.

Planting out The process of transferring a pot-raised plant into the ground outside.

Plumule The first shoot from the seed.

Polyembryonic A phenomenon whereby more than one shoot grows from a single seed and therefore into more than one plant.

Pruning The process of cutting back a plant to control its growth, both in terms of size and shape.

Radicle The first root from the seed.

Repotting The process of transferring a plant from one pot to another, usually bigger, pot. Or to refresh the compost for a plant remaining in the same pot.

Seed coat The skin of the seed, protecting the embryo and other parts of the seed inside. Its thickness and the chemicals it contains control how easily the seed will germinate.

Standard A plant trained and pruned with a clear single stem supporting a ball of branches and foliage, commonly pruned into a lollipop shape.

Viable A seed or pip that is capable of germinating and growing on.

FURTHER RESOURCES

For more information on growing, pruning and training fruit trees and bushes, pests and diseases, as well as comprehensive information on all aspects of (fruit and vegetable) gardening:

The website of The Royal Horticultural Society: www.rhs.org.uk

RHS Grow Your Own: For Kids by Chris Collins and Lia Leendertz (RHS/Mitchell Beazley, 2013

RHS Handbook: Garden Problem Solver by RHS (RHS/Mitchell Beazley, 2013)

RHS Handbook: Propagation Techniques by RHS (RHS/Mitchell Beazley, 2013)

RHS Handbook: Pruning and Training by RHS (RHS/Mitchell Beazley, 2013)

RHS Pests & Diseases by Pippa Greenwood and Andrew Halstead (RHS/Dorling Kindersley, 2007)

RHS Seeds: the ultimate guide to growing successfully from seed by Jekka McVicar (RHS/Kyle Cathie, 2008)

RHS Vegetable & Fruit Gardening by Michael Pollock (Ed.) (RHS/Dorling Kindersley, 2012)

To grow other plants from kitchen scraps and seed:

Asian Vegetables by Sally Cunningham (Eco-Logic Books, 2009)

Don't Throw It, Grow It! by Deborah Peterson and Millicent Selsam (Storey Publishing, 2008)

Local gardening groups and allotment societies offer resources and advice to new growers, and may be able to supply seeds of more unusual varieties.

Why not expand on the fruit and veg detailed here by trying the pips from produce found in specialist or ethnic greengrocers and markets?

INDEX

IMAGE CREDITS